Beating the Odds

The fall and rise of Bev Buckingham

Murray Mottram and
Bev Buckingham

ALLEN&UNWIN

First published in 2003

Copyright © Beverley Buckingham and Murray Mottram 2003

Allen & Unwin
83 Alexander Street
Crows Nest NSW 2065
Australia
Phone: (61 2) 8425 0100
Fax: (61 2) 9906 2218
Email: info@allenandunwin.com
Web: www.allenandunwin.com

National Library of Australia
Cataloguing-in-Publication entry:

Mottram, Murray.
  Beating the odds : the fall and rise of Bev Buckingham.

  Includes index.
  ISBN 1 74114 251 2.

  1. Buckingham, Bev. 2. Women jockeys - Australia -
Biography. I. Title.

798.40092

Set in 12.5/16.7 pt Bembo by Bookhouse, Sydney
Printed by Griffin Press, South Australia

10 9 8 7 6 5 4 3 2 1

Beating the Odds

Murray Mottram was born in Auckland, New Zealand, and began working as a journalist at the *New Zealand Herald* at the age of 17. He has lived in Melbourne since 1986, working for *The Age* as a writer and editor, and the *Sunday Age* as features editor and news editor.

His private passion is racing. He has shares in two horses, one of them taken up with the Buckinghams after finishing this book, and his dream is to have a horse good enough to win on Derby Day at Flemington.

Murray lives in Melbourne with his parter, Anne, and their two dogs.

Foreword

By John Tapp

I've never forgotten a wonderful racing telecast I saw in Tasmania in 1986. I was on holiday with family and friends and had just checked into a Devonport motel. I switched on the telly just in time to catch the running of the Hobart Cup in which Dark Intruder was the sentimental favourite, with the 'Queen of Tassie racing', Beverley Buckingham, in the saddle.

Although we were starved of Tasmanian racing news on the mainland, most enthusiasts were aware of the achievements of the fabulously successful female jockey. I can still see Bev dashing to the lead on Dark Intruder, leaving the back straight and adopting 'catch me if you can' tactics. The ride illustrated her understanding both of Dark Intruder and of the Elwick course. Bev got a rousing reception from the big crowd, which was warmed by the fact that she had just won the cup on a horse trained by her father, Ted.

I thought again of that day twelve years later when word of Bev's horrific race fall made the news bulletins around

Australia. I don't know how many times I'd considered asking her for an interview for the Nine Network during those intervening years, but I never seemed to find the time to travel to Tasmania.

It goes without saying that Bev was high on my guest list when Sky Racing introduced the 'Inside Racing' program in early 1999. She was sitting on the back verandah of the family home at Latrobe when I arrived with a camera crew, having already confounded her doctors by walking again, albeit tentatively. She was making rapid progress, but not rapid enough for a lady accustomed to controlling her own destiny. She was impatient; she was understandably bitter and struggling desperately to come to terms with the stark reality that she would never ride again.

The next time I saw Bev was later that year on the set of 'This Is Your Life' at Nine's Melbourne studio. She was in a buoyant mood as she greeted family and friends from home and overseas.

Our third meeting was just before Christmas 2002 when I visited the Buckinghams' newly acquired property at Benalla, in Victoria, where Ted has a small team of horses in work. The difference in Bev was astounding. She was poised and confident, very focused and giving as much as she got from Mum, Dad and staff.

Much had happened in her life since our previous interview almost four years earlier—a broken marriage, a darling little daughter, a move to the mainland and tremendous progress in her rehabilitation. I struggled with a lump in my throat as I watched Bev climb onto the back of a massively overweight Clydesdale mare called Dolly, and head out onto a small exercise track. She rose to the trot and for a short time rolled into a canter. She was in complete control and you could tell that old Dolly respected and liked the lady on her back. I was suddenly struck with the realisation that this remarkable young woman had been the most successful female jockey in Australian history when her career was cut so tragically short.

When I had arrived at the Buckingham property that morning, I had been instantly taken by an imposing ash tree near the house and had expressed my admiration of it to Bev's mother, Joan. On leaving some hours later, Joan presented me with two tiny potted seedlings of the majestic ash. I planted both on my property on the outskirts of Sydney and kept the water up during some heatwave conditions over Christmas and New Year. One of them didn't make it, but the other has thrived and looks certain to attain the grandeur of its parent.

My wife Ann and I have already christened that young ash 'The Buckingham Tree', and as it grows it symbolises the life of a remarkable young woman. Every leaf represents one of the million tears shed by Bev, Joan and Ted during the darkest hours. The far-reaching boughs represent the many horizons Bev conquered during her golden days in the saddle, and that sturdy trunk symbolises the courage and strength of spirit with which she faced every challenge, on and off the racetrack.

John Tapp
Senior presenter, Sky Racing, March 2003

For Mum and Dad,
who were always there for me,
and for Tara,
who made me happy again
—BB

Contents

PART ONE

THE FALL

The fall

It didn't hurt when I broke my neck.

I knew there would be damage—there always will be when you fall off a racehorse going more than 50 kilometres an hour. But even as I hurtled towards the Elwick racecourse turf, I wasn't panicking.

I'd been in worse spills before. Tossed metres into the air, landing head first, knocked out cold. Dragged along by my thumb tangled in a horse's mane until it was pulled clean out of the socket. (Now *that* hurt!)

This time I was as relaxed as you can be when you slam into the ground under a 500-kilogram thoroughbred. I heard no cracking of bone, felt no burst of pain. Nothing.

My mental faculties were working fine. I instantly calculated that in two more strides the flailing legs of the oncoming horse would crash into my chest. Instinctively, my brain sent my body a message to roll out of the way. The signal didn't get past my shoulder blades. Not a single muscle moved.

Luckily those metal-tipped hooves missed my chest. Instead they churned through the flesh of my left thigh, gouging out a wound that would take 40 stitches to put back together.

I didn't feel a thing.

When you watch the TV replay of my fall, you can see clearly how me, and my life, were turned on their head.

It's Saturday 30 May, 1998. The field in the Cheaper Liquor Company Maiden Plate has travelled about 350 metres down the back straight at Elwick, Hobart's main racecourse. I've managed to slot my mount, Theutelle, into the perfect position behind the leader, Glitterati Affair. As we begin the turn out of the straight, Glitterati Affair's jockey, Bruce MacDonald, slackens the pace.

My hands squeeze back on the reins. Those thin leather straps are a jockey's lifeline in this situation. The adrenaline pumping through Theutelle's veins—and hundreds of years of inbreeding—are telling her to run like hell. My tug on the reins, pulling back on the bit in her mouth, is a message to her brain to override all that instinct and excitement. Unless she gets that message we are going to slam straight into Glitterati Affair's rump.

I liked to think I was as strong as any male jockey, but the fact is no 52-kilo human is going to pull up a charging horse that is ten times heavier unless the beast cooperates. And Theutelle is not cooperating. Instead of tucking her head to her chest and shortening her stride, she fights my gentle command.

The fall

Now put the replay on slow motion: Theutelle's head dips, then rises vertically like a rocking horse. Her front legs have clipped the heels of Glitterati Affair and she's scrambling to stay on her feet. But it's too late. Theutelle's back legs crumple underneath her and she goes into an uncontrollable, stumbling slide.

This yanks me up out of the saddle onto her neck. I slide down the near side, my arms reaching up for her head and my legs grasping for the underside of her neck. In the last few frames, before we merge with the earth, I'm facing straight up at the sky, curled into the shape of an unborn child.

My point of impact with the ground is right between the shoulder blades, with my legs still in the air. This is the exact moment when two bones in my neck get broken.

The bones, or vertebrae, sit on top of each other like a stack of chairs. What enables them to bend and turn are the discs between them—slivers of jelly-like tissue that act as lubricant and shock absorber. The force of landing on the top of my spine slams two vertebrae together, squeezing the disc between them into the spinal cord.

The spinal cord runs down the middle of the vertebrae. It's the communications line carrying messages to and from the brain and the limbs. Now the line is down. The message to roll away to safety can't get through from my brain to my body. Pain—the emergency call from injured areas—can't get from my body to my brain.

The second thing to hit the ground is my head, which then snaps back up like a jack-in-the-box on a spring. This sends another shockwave down the spinal cord. Now the line is not only down but tangled.

With all communication cut off or scrambled just below the level of my chin, about the only thing I can do is breathe. Maybe that's why it seems so quiet as I lie there on the soft grass, blinking at the clouds, paralysed but feeling no pain. Just the wind on my face and my own breathing.

Right then, I didn't know anything about the complex and fragile make-up of the spinal cord—that wouldn't be fully explained to me until weeks later. All I knew was that there was something badly wrong that was stopping me from moving. I wasn't frightened. Maybe my body had just gone into shock, I thought. The word 'quadriplegic' certainly didn't enter my head.

The two ambulance officers at the track were quickly on the scene.

'Are you alright?' one of them asked.

'No, I can't move anything,' I said.

They tested for movement and feeling in my arms and legs. I could raise my upper arms off the ground but that was about all, they had no real power. The tips of the outside three fingers of both hands were numb, a classic sign of spinal nerve damage. The only feeling in my legs was a pins and needles sensation below the knees and in my feet. They wouldn't move at all.

Otherwise I was fine—I scored 15 out of 15 on the Glasgow Coma Score, the basic test for concussion or head injury. Eyes opening spontaneously: four out of four. Talking lucidly: five out of five. Responding to commands: six out of six.

Pulse, temperature and breathing: all normal.

The paramedics called for back-up from the Goodwood Road station a couple of minutes away. They wanted two extra pairs of hands to make the delicate lift onto their special spinal support stretcher before placing me in the ambulance. Paul Davy, the first paramedic on the scene, held my head and neck as his three colleagues helped to 'log-roll' me onto my side, allowing the spinal board to slide in underneath my back. Paul says my neck was so smashed up it felt like a bean bag full of broken glass.

Michael Loughead, the retired head of the intensive care unit at Royal Hobart Hospital and a keen racegoer, was in the grandstand with his binoculars on Theutelle when she went down. He raced to the stewards' room and jumped in their car as they headed off to the accident scene. Paul Davy quickly briefed him. 'Spinal damage, looks bad.'

Loughead rang the Royal Hobart and put the neuro-surgery ward on notice. 'Incoming functional quadriplegic, put surgical team on standby.'

As the ambulance left the course, the crew hooked me up to an electro-cardiograph machine to monitor my heart rate. A strong heartbeat is important for a spinal cord injury. With all the rest of the damage, you don't want blood build-ing up around the injured area adding to the traffic jam—you want it flowing through, bringing as much oxygen as poss-ible to the damaged cells.

When we left Elwick for the hospital, my blood pressure was normal at 120 over 80. But there's a funny thing about the way the brain regulates the heart. The signal for speeding up the heart rate is sent down the spinal cord. The signal for slowing it down comes via a nerve system in the side of the neck. My heart's accelerator cable was cut and it was only getting messages from its brakes. By the time we got to the hospital my blood pressure had dropped to 110—not critical, but not helpful.

Just before we pulled up at the Royal Hobart's accident and emergency ward, I heard one of the paramedics say something about stemming the flow of blood.

'What do you mean, blood?' I said.

I couldn't feel or see any. Then he told me about the gash in my leg. I still didn't believe it—if I could feel pins and needles, surely I'd notice a 15-centimetre gash in my thigh. I started to argue, so they showed me a section of my torn white riding pants, dyed crimson with blood. That's when I started to get really worried.

At 12.44 p.m. I was delivered to cubicle R1 in the accident and emergency ward. By then I was having some trouble breathing. I couldn't spread my fingers and had decreased sensation from the ribs down. The initial hospital admission report tells me all this but doesn't record my name, so perhaps now is the time to fill in the missing biographical details.

In May 1998 I was 33 years old, married for just over a year.

I'd been a jockey since I left school at fourteen. In that time I'd established myself as Australia's most successful lady rider. I was the first woman in the world to win a state jockeys' premiership. I'd kicked home more than 900 winners, won the Tasmanian State Premiership three times, beaten the best jockeys on the mainland and represented my country overseas.

Don't get me wrong—I wasn't on any crusade for women's liberation. I just believed that no matter who you are, if you're capable of doing a job you shouldn't be barred from making a living at it because of your gender, age, size, race or religion.

I was pretty strong-willed by nature, but the prejudice I struck when I started riding made me all the more determined to prove the doubters wrong. After eighteen years I'd silenced even the crustiest old-school blokes of the Tasmanian racing industry. I was a local hero in my home State. I'd had songs written about me and barely a week went by when I wasn't in the sports pages or on TV. My accident made the papers in Melbourne, Sydney and Brisbane.

I loved horses, I loved race riding, and although I felt I was in peak form, I knew there was still improvement left in me. For the past two years I'd run second in the State jockeys' race and I was determined to get the title back. With two months of the racing season to go I was on top of the table.

Away from the track, life was great. I had just come back from a holiday in Queensland with my husband, Jason, and two close friends, Kim and Lenny Dixon. Kim and I had been trailblazers in the early 1980s as part of the first batch of girls to ride professionally against men. Over the years we'd become like sisters, with all the arguments and periods of not talking that goes with being so close.

Jason and I had been married only thirteen months, but we had been together for three and a half years before that.

I loved him to bits. We lived with my parents, Ted and Joan Buckingham—the two most important people in my life—on the family horse-training property at Latrobe, in north-western Tasmania. Jason helped around the stable.

Jason and I had plans to start a family, but not straight away. I wanted to work and travel overseas before settling down. We'd talked about me riding in Singapore the following year.

Longer term, I wanted to retire within five years, then spend six months seeing the world with Jason, who had never been overseas. I wanted to go to England to see the extended family I'd never met—Mum and Dad had migrated to Australia when I was two. Then we'd go to Europe, see the great historic sights of Italy, eat the great food of France. Maybe stop in Egypt on the way home and take each other's picture standing in front of the pyramids, or stop over at Disneyland and get shots of us with Mickey Mouse and Goofy instead.

After I had that out of my system I'd be ready to have children. Once they were under control I would take over training the horses and Dad could retire. Officially that is—from the day I started my jockey's apprenticeship under him, Dad and I had been 'The Team' and that wouldn't change just because he'd handed over the training reins.

Ted, Joan, Bev, Jason and the kids would all live happily ever after.

That was the plan, anyway.

Mum was at home listening to the races on the radio when Theutelle crashed to the ground, snapping her left foreleg and bringing three other horses down.

These are the moments every jockey's family dreads, the empty minutes between the commentator calling the fall and the finish of the race, when he turns the binoculars back to the scene of the accident to report on the casualties.

I'd had plenty of falls before. I'd had broken ribs, cracked wrists, a busted shoulder, bruised internal organs and all manner of sprains, strains, torn muscles and bruises the colour of boot polish. As soon as the injury healed I was back to work without a second thought. As the saying goes, you've just got to get straight back on the horse.

Mum didn't come to the races much. With Dad, Jason and I there every week someone needed to be at home to keep the stable ticking over, and she worried so much about my safety she couldn't really enjoy watching me ride in the flesh.

We had an arrangement that if I did fall I would sit up on the track as soon as I had collected my breath so the race caller could see I was OK. This time, of course, I couldn't. The caller was able to report that the other three riders who had come down, Dean Larsson, Simon Snell and Melissa Brunton, were all on their feet. The ambulance men were still hovering over me fifteen minutes after the crash. Mum's throat went dry.

She rang the racecourse but no one could tell her anything. She tried to ring Dad, who was out watching Jason play football. Dad had just got back from holidays and didn't have a horse running that day.

Jason's team was playing in the sticks, out of mobile phone range. Mum rang the nearest police station and asked them to go and find him. Meanwhile, Dad was sitting in his car, parked on the edge of the footy oval. He'd listened to the race on the radio too, but he wasn't as concerned as Mum. He'd seen me pick myself up off the deck too often to believe this time would be any different. That was until the police officer tapped on his car window.

As he drove towards home Dad kept dialling Mum until he got a connection. She'd rung the racecourse again and still no one could tell her how I was, only that I was on my way to Royal Hobart Hospital. Dad tried to assure her I'd be all right but it wasn't working. When he got out of the car she was half-way down the garden path. 'Maybe it's just a broken arm,' he said. He packed some clothes and headed off on the three-hour drive to Hobart. Mum got back on the phone to the hospital.

Dianne Parish, a fellow jockey and one of my closest and dearest friends, beat Dad to my bedside. She came straight from the track with my gear from my locker, expecting to pick me up and drive me home. She's such an optimist.

By the time Dad got to the Royal Hobart I'd had a spinal x-ray and CAT scan. They showed I had fractured the C3 and C5 vertebrae in my neck—the third and fifth bones from the top of the stack. The damage to the fifth bone was the worst, with three small pieces having broken off.

The real problem was the disc between the fifth and sixth vertebrae. It's hard to believe that something the size of a five-cent piece, with the consistency of an oyster, could bring 99 per cent of a human body to a dead halt. Well, it can. The disc wedged into my spinal cord had only been displaced by about half a centimetre, but that was enough to crush the communication line into near silence. The initial impact and resulting whiplash effect had caused bruising and swelling of the spinal cord above and below the protruding disc. I'd also fractured my top left rib, which sits just above the lung.

It was great to see Dad walk into the emergency ward. My biggest worry—apart from the obvious—was the panic and stress Mum and Jason must have been feeling as they waited at home for Dad to get to the hospital and tell them what the real situation was.

Dad leaned over the bed and gave me a cuddle. That gave me more comfort than the two doses of morphine I'd had by then.

'It's not good,' I said to Dad. 'I can't feel anything in my legs.'

Dad made the standard comforting comments—'Don't worry, we'll get you out of here, I'm here for you.'

A doctor came in and tapped Dad on the shoulder. He wanted to talk to him outside. The doctor outlined the extent of my injuries. He wanted Dad to give his permission for an operation to remove the displaced disc. Hopefully that would remove the blockage in the spinal cord and allow a return to normal transmission.

Dad agreed and about half an hour later I was drifting off into the spooky dreamland of anaesthetics and painkillers that would be my world for the next two weeks.

Cut to the bone

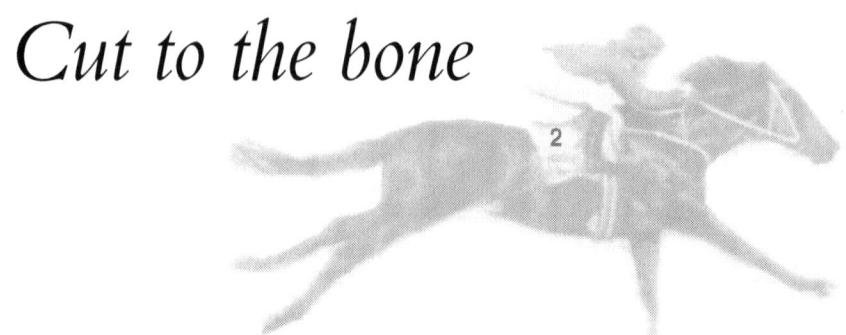

2

The three surgeons were tooled up like a team of safe breakers.

They had closely studied the structural plans of my spine: x-rays of the bone damage and magnetic resonance image (MRI) scans of the tissue trauma. From the x-rays the untrained eye would not see much to worry about, just a few thin, shadowy lines marking the fractures and a tiny piece of chipped bone floating free. On the MRI pictures the problem is obvious. The scan is literally a blueprint—the bones and spinal cord register sea-blue on the scan prints and the discs come out darker, almost black. The surgeons, led by the experienced consultant Dr John Liddell, were surprised by the bulging blob of black strangling my spinal cord. Usually it's bone that pierces the cord—surgeons rarely see the gooey, gelatinous inside of a disc burst out of its stringy casing and into the spinal canal.

The good news was that although the escaped inside of the disc had crushed the spinal cord in half it hadn't cut through it, which meant that if they could remove the pressure point I had a good chance of recovering plenty of limb function.

The operation had its risks, though. The longer the blood flow to the injury site was blocked, the greater the chance of permanent damage. My blood pressure was already down and the effects of a general anaesthetic would keep it subdued. The surgical team would have to get in and out as quickly as possible, removing the most prized item—the burst disc— and not worrying about anything else.

The trio—Liddell, his senior registrar, Dr James van Gelder, and an assistant—checked off their equipment: cutting implements, tick; high-speed drill, tick; mechanical saw, tick; operating microscope, tick.

Liddell gave the signal for van Gelder to make the first cut. Van Gelder pressed his razor-sharp scalpel onto the right-hand side of my throat, half-way between the Adam's apple and the back of the neck. The rubbery flesh parted bloodlessly as he sliced across a few centimetres, opening a direct approach to the front of the spinal column.

Inside the throat, the food and wind pipes dangled to the side of the incision. They were pulled back out of the way. To the left was the carotid artery, which carries blood to the brain. To make the opening big enough to work in, retractors—like a carpenter's vice, only in reverse—were placed in the wound and pulled out to form an opening the size of a 50-cent piece.

Using an image intensifier (a portable x-ray machine), Liddell took new shots to make sure the exterior x-rays hadn't missed anything and to identify the target site for the next and most delicate phase, cutting the burst disc off the cord.

Liddell checked the blood pressure reading. The anaesthetist was feeding me noradrenaline, a stimulant that occurs naturally in the brain, promoting blood flow to the spinal cord to counter the effects of the anaesthetic. So far, so good.

Now the microscope, with a bright light attached, was focused into my throat cavity. Looking through the eye pieces, van Gelder now had under his nose the unlikely Crown jewel—a slimy wedge of disc tissue, embedded in some of the most complex and fragile circuitry in the human body.

Slowly, carefully, he lowered his longuers, an elongated pair of tweezers, and began pulling out blobs of disc. Millimetre by millimetre, the spinal cord opened out to its full width.

Finally, when he had removed all the disc material, a soft pulsing could be seen along the outer casing of my spinal cord, marking the return of blood flow to the injury site. The team could relax for a minute—the toughest task was over. They had emptied the safe without tripping the alarm.

Using a metal hook, similar to that used by dentists seeking out cavities, van Gelder probed around the back of my vertebrae to check there was no more disc material to be removed. All clear.

Now for phase two: inserting a bone graft into the space left by the extracted disc, so that the spinal column would stay in its correct alignment.

With the high-speed drill, again similar to a dentist's, van Gelder buffed off the tissue on the facing surfaces of the fifth and sixth vertebrae—one of the keys to a successful graft is to have direct bone-to-bone contact.

The most suitable bone to graft on to vertebrae comes from the hip. The shape of the hip suits the requirements for the graft: hard bone on three sides to give strength, and soft, cancellous bone—the spongy inner part—on the other to meld with the bone it is wedged against.

Van Gelder made another scalpel cut, down my right hip. Then he took a small, air-powered mechanical saw and cut away a disc-sized piece of bone. That was then slotted into the gap left by the missing disc.

With my type of injury, the new bone would usually be backed up by a metal brace screwed in to the vertebrae above and below the graft to give the repaired area extra strength. However, Liddell was conscious of the clock—he wanted to keep my time under anaesthetic to a minimum.

More than two hours after van Gelder made his first cut, Liddell signalled for the neck and hip wounds to be suctioned out and stitched.

Dad was waiting anxiously outside the theatre when the doctors emerged.

They told him the operation had gone well. However, the tests taken after the surgery—to see if I could tell the difference between a pin and a finger pressed into my fingers and toes—had not shown much change from beforehand. It seemed there may be permanent damage to the spinal cord. There was no guarantee I would ever walk again.

Dad didn't give anything away when he came in to see me around midnight. I was awake but still pretty drowsy.

He told me the doctors were pleased with the operation. He said not to worry—he was going to sleep in a room right next to my ward. If anything happened during the night he'd be there. After a few minutes I drifted off again.

When I woke up at 7.30 a.m. the nurse tested my movement and feeling. I could lift my upper arms by flexing my shoulder muscles, but I had no control below the elbows. I could make my hands move slightly by flexing my wrists. My thumbs and forefingers wiggled very slightly. My legs wouldn't budge at all, although I could feel a dull sensation when the nurse pressed into my calf or thigh muscles.

There was one thing I could feel perfectly—the pain in my neck. Removing the disc may not have cleared the communication lines for movement commands, but the channel for pain was well and truly open for business. Hot, throbbing pain. Pain so strong I couldn't concentrate on breathing, which was now a constant effort.

Late in the morning visitors started to arrive. Bruce Mac-Donald, Glitterati Affair's jockey, came in saying he felt terrible, although he hadn't thought he'd done anything wrong. He hadn't. I'd crossed to the lead and slowed the pace in a race a hundred times, just the way he had. I told him not to worry. (When the stewards later held an inquiry into the fall, they found that no rider was responsible—a result I'm perfectly happy with.)

Then Mum and Jason arrived. Mum hadn't known what to expect and was taken aback at seeing me having a laugh with Bruce. The way I understood things at that moment— or the way I *chose* to understand things—was that I had a 'broken neck'. Broken bones heal. Sure, I was in a bad way, but once those broken bones mended I would get back to work, riding winners.

I wouldn't quite be ready to ride the next Saturday though, so I went through our likely runners with Dad, telling him which jockeys I thought would suit which horses.

Greg Richardson, a racehorse owner who Dad trained for and who had become a close family friend, was there. He had driven Mum and Jason down to Hobart. Rod Clingeleffer, the chairman of the Tasmanian Racing Club, also dropped in.

We knew there would be a queue of media inquiries about my condition and requests to talk to the family, but none of us were up to it. We asked Greg, who was a lawyer, to look after that for us. As the bell sounded for the end of visiting hours, Greg got up to leave. I could see he was close to tears. 'Greg, come back here,' I said. 'I *will* walk out of here.'

At that stage I even believed it.

That night my breathing got weaker and weaker. The spinal damage had caused a loss of diaphragm power. On top of this, the morphine I had been given as pain relief was suppressing my breathing. The combination of this and the fact I had to lie flat on my back or on my side meant I couldn't cough up the secretions in my chest. My 40-a-day smoking habit of the past fifteen years didn't help either. I had to have a suction tube inserted every couple of hours to clear my airways.

The doctors were getting concerned. They ordered another set of chest x-rays and I was propped up at a 45-degree angle for a while to see if that would help me clear my chest before I went to sleep.

As the night went on my breathing got worse. The base of both lungs had collapsed, worse in the right one than the left. At 3 a.m. the supervising doctor ordered that I be transferred to the intensive care unit to be fitted to a mechanical breathing system. A plastic tube was inserted down my breathing passage. This connected to a ventilator, which pushed oxygen into my lungs and then sucked up the carbon dioxide I exhaled.

When I woke up there was good news and bad news. The good news was I wouldn't feel so tired and distressed from poor oxygen supply. The bad news was the tube down my throat stopped my vocal cords from moving so I couldn't talk.

It hardly mattered. The anaesthetic for the operation, the morphine for the pain, the dopamine to make my heart beat faster and the midazolam to keep me sedated had me asleep or in a daze most of the time. Mum, Dad and Jason came in to see me, but nothing they said really registered.

Dr Liddell planned to send me to the Austin Hospital in Melbourne, which has a specialist spinal cord injury unit, when I had recovered from the operation. The Austin didn't have a bed available straight away and besides, I couldn't travel until my respiratory system had stabilised. So for the next 36 hours I just lay there being pumped full of oxygen and drugs, alive but barely conscious, in limbo between the happy and successful life I'd known and the uncertain, tormented one I was about to discover.

Dad was at home on Wednesday, four days after the fall, when the call came through. I was being airlifted to Melbourne that afternoon. There were tickets waiting for Dad and Jason at Devonport airport, a few minutes' drive from home, on a commercial flight. They should pack their bags, get to the airport and head for the Austin Hospital once they touched down in Melbourne.

They were at the Austin when my ambulance arrived but I was too sedated to notice. They took turns to sit next to my bed in the intensive care ward, whispering words of comfort when I came to because the painkillers had worn off or the breathing tube had become clogged with what the nurses described as 'thick, creamy offensive-smelling sputum'.

The next morning I had a new round of x-rays and scans. It didn't look good. The ligaments running along the back and sides of my spine had been so badly damaged that they could not properly support it. The stack of chairs was in danger of toppling over.

The trip over Bass Strait in a state of semi-consciousness had upset me. When I wasn't in a restless sleep, I was in tears of intermittent, chronic pain, disorientation and frustration.

The next batch of x-rays and scans the following day brought more bad news. The vertebrae directly above where the disc had been cut away had shifted. The curve of the neck bones was out of alignment and was at risk of causing further damage to the spinal cord. I would have to have another operation to lock the bones into their right place.

This time the surgeon came in the back way to my broken neck.

I was placed face down on the operating table, which had a special device to hold my head in place called, appropriately enough, a horseshoe. This is an attachment at the head of the table, a bit like the hole for your face in a massage table. The semi-circular 'horseshoe' cups under the patient's head, supporting the pressure of the surgeon working on the back of the neck. Under general anaesthetic you're not going to feel the cold, solid surface of the horseshoe on your nose and eye sockets, but they put padding on it anyway so you don't wake up with a sore face on top of everything else.

Before the surgeon, Dr Peter Wilde, got down to business his assistants shaved the back of my head so stray hairs didn't fall in while I was opened up. The nurses swabbed the skin from the base of my skull to my shoulders with alcoholic iodine to disinfect the surface. Now Wilde was ready to make his first cut.

He traced a 15-centimetre slice down the middle of my neck. Then he peeled the muscles between the neck and the shoulders away from the vertebrae. You've probably done a similar thing to get to the tasty bits of an orange: pressing your thumbs into the middle and pulling the segments to either side to expose the soft, white core.

Now Wilde could see for himself, through the powerful pair of magnifying glasses perched on the end of his nose, the problem the scans had revealed. The ligaments at my fourth and fifth vertebrae were ruptured and frayed, providing no support to the 'stack' and therefore making it unstable.

To compensate for this lack of external support, the plan was to place a titanium plate on either side of the fourth, fifth and six vertebrae to hold them in place. The plates would be attached to the bones with screws, exactly the same way you would join two pieces of timber with a bracket. They used to use stainless steel for the plates, but it blocks the MRI, making it hard for doctors to monitor the injured areas with follow-up scans after surgery. So now titanium is used, because it is readily accepted by body tissue and is see-through for MRI scans.

Like a carpentry repair job, Wilde started by cleaning the surfaces to be joined. In my case, this meant scraping the soft tissue away from the vertebrae and smoothing off any sharp edges of bone. He placed the titanium plates—about one centimetre wide and four centimetres long—in position, then secured them with screws, top and bottom. Wilde didn't risk putting screws into the middle bone, the one with the worst fractures, for fear of shattering it.

All that remained to complete the job was filling the cracks with fragments of bone from my hip—human poly-filler, if you like. Dr Wilde made a new cut down to my left hip bone and chipped out a few slivers with a small hammer and chisel. He grafted these into the cracks in the back of the bones in my neck. It didn't matter that they weren't quite a perfect fit; natural bone growth would gradually knit them together.

With this reinforcement at the side and back of the vertebrae, on top of the bone graft at the front I'd had in Hobart, my neck was now stronger than before it was broken. But that didn't fix the all-important spinal cord inside it, still swollen, tangled and, as far as my arms and legs were concerned, off the air.

Morphine dreams

Morphine is named after the Greek god of dreams, Morpheus. This handy byproduct of the opium poppy has been put to great use as a painkiller in hospitals and on battlefields over the years. It works by neutralising the chemicals in the brain that register physical pain. If you process morphine a bit more you get heroin, the drug of choice for those trying to obliterate emotional pain. Junkies would have killed for the supply of morphine I was getting.

The day of the second operation I was having five milligrams of morphine and three or four milligrams of midazolam, a powerful sedative, pumped into my veins every hour. This kept me in the state heroin addicts crave: oblivious to all the hurt—physical and emotional—of the real world.

In the days after the metal plates were fitted to my spine the doctors lowered the dosage so that I wasn't out of it all the time. Like a junkie, as soon as the drugs wore off I was able to feel all the pain and desperation they took away. I got panicky.

Paranoid even. The nursing notes record—with an exclamation mark denoting disbelief—that at one point I was refusing to swallow because I thought my saliva was poisonous.

A lot of little things were building up my stress levels. The breathing tube down my throat was driving me crazy. The sticky tape holding it in place around my mouth gave me a maddening itch. I could hear the sputum gurgling away in the breathing pipe and see condensation in the tube that ran from my mouth to the ventilator, my 'iron lungs'. I was convinced I was going to drown in my body's own liquids.

I didn't have the capacity to pull the tube out with my hands, although I did have a crack at knocking the damn thing out by throwing the dead weight of my forearms against it.

Like a true junkie, I became very cunning at getting what I needed. Using my tongue and vocal cords I managed to dislodge the tube. I was so persistent at flopping my arms on the tube and spitting it out using my tongue that some nurses tied my hands to the bed. When they went to push the tube back down my throat, I bit through it.

Only the morphine and midazolam could bring me, and the nurses, any peace.

Midazolam puts you to sleep in a hypnotic-like state and can cause hallucinations. Used together with morphine it produces a perfect combination for studying Freud's theories on the workings of the subconscious.

My use of morphine and midazolam, as with most drug habits, started off quite pleasurably. The first drug-dream I recall clearly must have come during or after the airlift from Hobart. In the dream I had the power to control the plane with my mind—which was a good thing because the plane was falling from the sky, largely due to the double horse float in the back. Dad had won the float as a prize in a golf tournament. The pilot opened the back of the plane and dumped the float. With that, and my paranormal powers over the joystick, the plane was able to climb back to its proper cruising altitude.

That dream, I suppose, combined the turbulence I'd experienced on the flight across Bass Strait with the great time I had playing golf in Queensland just before the fall. (Over the years I'd played the odd round of golf for fun but this time I had got hooked. One of the first things I had done when I got home from South Molle Island was buy a set of clubs. And Dad was always winning prizes at golf tournaments, although never anything as useful as a horse float.)

The dream had a sequel at the Austin Hospital. I was in my bed on the roof of the hospital and there were lots of planes flying past, in danger of crashing. With my amazing new psychic powers, I was able to keep them safely aloft. As 'Super Bev' nursed the faltering jet liners through the sky and around the hospital buildings, Kim Dixon's husband, Lenny, appeared and started taking bets on whether the planes would crash or not. He knew I wouldn't let them fall, so he collected big time from the pessimists among the crowd that had gathered to witness my astonishing powers. (Lenny is known for loving a bargain.)

In another dream, which must have occurred around the time of the second neck operation, I was lying on a very long wooden table. Suddenly I was flung right to the end of it like a glass of whisky sliding the length of a bar in one of those old cowboy movies. Only I kept going, off the end and onto the floor. I already had a broken neck. When my head crashed onto the floor my neck broke again and that, in the dream, was why I required another operation.

I don't know if you could call it a dream, but I also recall a sort of vision of myself in Dad's lap. 'Please fix me up, make me better,' I said. For once he couldn't.

The next wave of dreams were worse. In these episodes I'd been flown to an island with a hospital on it. (Maybe this was a flashback to the holiday at South Molle.) My husband Jason was there. He was playing up with a Filipino woman, who was about 45 and worked as a nurse on the island.

I have no idea where this stuff came from. I had never had any reason to suspect Jason of cheating on me. And when I first saw Jason walk into the intensive care ward at the Austin, I'd cried tears of relief. But the dream was so vivid that when I came to I didn't want Dad to let Jason in to see me again.

This dream also had a sequel. This time I was a hostage on the island. The nurses were holding me captive. I had to sit tight and wait for an opportunity for my friend Kim to rescue me. I'd pretend to be sleeping and she would sneak in to get me out.

Kim featured in another dream; she was lying over me to protect me from darts raining down from above. I was on the floor and there were people in the roof firing darts at me. Kim took them all in her back.

Then the really dark stuff began. People were trying to kill me. Everyone was against me except my family. Mum and Dad were on my side, but they had to fly to England for some reason. Kim was there defending me. Jason was on the sidelines, looking on, neither for me nor against me.

The Filipino woman reappeared. She was in the ward with me, all alone. She leaned over with a cigarette and burned it into my shoulder. She was taunting me about sleeping with Jason. Her hands went to my mouth as if to suffocate me. There was only one thing I could do—bite her hand with all my might. My teeth sank into her flesh until they hit bone. I had a good long think about whether I should keep going and bite right through. I decided not to.

But this was no mere dream. My victim was, in fact, an Asian nurse who had tied my hands down quite roughly and reinserted my ejected ventilator tube while I was semi-conscious. Suddenly I was wide awake with my teeth down to the bone on her thumb. If there was any doubt this was real life, the terrified expression on her face dispelled it. Later I heard she needed stitches in her thumb wound, but I never got to apologise. Somehow she never came back to work on my ward again.

After two weeks the dreams became out-and-out night-mares. I was trapped in a cage, naked. I couldn't stand up. There were other people in cages as well. They were prisoners, too.

In the worst version, I got out of the cage only to find it was one of a series of cages, or rooms, in a huge maze. In a creepy version of *Mission Impossible* I had to go through a series of procedures—push a button, pull on a lever or tread on a certain spot—to get into the next room. I only had a few seconds. An explosion, a roof falling in—something— was going to kill me if I didn't get out in time. I must have been having this nightmare around midnight on 11 June, twelve days after the fall. The nurse's notes record me waking in fright, mouthing, 'Don't kill me please.' The cage nightmare got so bad that I asked for the doctors to take me off morphine—I'd rather put up with the shooting neck pains any day.

Playing Sigmund Freud for a minute, I think I can work these nightmares out. They probably occurred just after the titanium plate surgery. The 'cage' could be the horseshoe attachment and all the monitoring equipment I was plugged into. The other people could be the rest of the patients in intensive care. Being naked might be my subconscious recalling my being undressed before being draped in the surgical gown I wore during the operation. Or maybe it was more abstract, a metaphor for feeling vulnerable. I couldn't have known it then, but the maze nightmare was a pretty good prophecy of the next five years. One by one the rooms that housed my life blew apart. First my body, then my spirit was demolished. Even my marriage—the one place in which I thought I could safely take refuge—would cave in on me.

So it's interesting now to look back on the characters in my nightmares and the roles they played. Mum and Dad supporting me, but unable to heal my wounds. Kim protecting me. And Jason fooling around with another woman.

The waking nightmare

4

An intensive care unit is a bit like a casino. The lights never go out so you never know whether it's night or day. It's full of people down on their luck. They sit in tight huddles, stony-faced, trying to convince themselves their fortunes are going to take a turn for the better any minute now. They're in what psychologists call denial.

To win my way out of intensive care I had to beat the house at two simple games—breathing without the ventilator and swallowing a blue dye without letting any into my lungs.

Once the morphine and midazolam doses had been lowered and I was able to really comprehend the state my body was in, I wanted to start winning, and quickly. I realised that I was relying on machines for every basic function; to breathe for me, feed me, remove my waste.

Since my fall I'd been fed solely on a brownish mixture designed to supply my daily energy, protein and liquid requirements. I don't know what it tasted like—it came in through a tube in my nose that delivered it straight to the front door of my stomach, bypassing my taste buds. For fifteen years I had waged a weekly battle to ride at 52 kilos. After a fortnight on this diet I'd dropped to 45.

The wasting away to skin and bone accentuated the swelling of my stomach after the second operation due to a build-up of internal gas. A tube was inserted into my rectum to try to alleviate the discomfort. My bowels emptied themselves periodically without warning. I was as helpless as a child in nappies. A tube connected to my bladder drained off my urine.

The nurses washed me with wet sponges. It took a few days after the second operation before I had my hair washed for the first time since the fall. It was still speckled with dirt and blood and Mum pestered the nurses to do something about it. I remember the lovely, soft feeling of the shampoo and the fingers rubbing my scalp. Little treats like that make a big difference when you are in the condition I was in.

Because I couldn't move my head, I had to wear a special pair of glasses to watch the TV at the foot of the bed. They had two sets of lenses joined in a V-shape. The ones facing the TV bounced the picture onto the ones at the end of my nose, facing my eyes.

I could hear the sound fine. In fact the one thing that improved out of sight in intensive care was my hearing. I suppose because I couldn't talk or move my only way of connecting with the outside world was listening. My hearing got so keen I could keep track of four conversations at once—Mum talking to Kim, the people talking in the cubicle next door, the nurses talking outside and TV dialogue down the corridor.

If you don't use your muscles it doesn't take long for them to forget what they are there for. Calf stimulators were applied to remind my leg muscles of what they would be doing if I was on my feet. My fingers, cut off from their central command post, curled up like the petals of a flower at sundown. To stop them becoming frozen in the shape of claws I had hand splints fitted to stretch them out straight.

The splints were pretty solid and made dangerous weapons. One time I went to scratch my brow—my shoulder muscles could raise my upper arms off the bed for the first part of the move, but I had no power in my triceps to control the lowering of the hand to the forehead. My forearm, loaded up with the splints, succumbed to the law of gravity and crashed down onto my face.

To stop pressure sores forming on my back I was turned every few hours—'log rolling' it's called—from my back to one side, to the other side, then on to my back again. With a neck collar holding my head rigidly in position I had three alternate views: the plain white ceiling for four hours; the various machines keeping me alive on one side for the next two hours; then two hours staring at the curtain around my cubicle.

I had a special mechanical bed that folded in on itself so that rather than being rolled on a flat mattress I would be turned by the bed itself—a bit like a rotisserie chicken. For quite a while it produced a weird feeling of vertigo during the periods on my side—I always felt as though I was going to fall out onto the floor.

Because the lights were always on and I was being moved so often I slept in fits, day and night, never quite knowing which was which.

At least in a casino you can drink away the pain. My neck still ached from the surgery. Panadeine Forte didn't provide the relief of morphine, but putting up with some extra pain was better than dealing with the nightmares.

So you can understand why I was keen to get out of intensive care. To do that I had to prove I could breathe for myself and that I could ingest solid food and drink without letting it get into my lungs. My respiratory function had been severely weakened by the damage to my nervous system and the drugs I'd been fed. My gag, or cough reflex, was not strong enough to bring up out of the lungs anything that spilled in from the entrance to the stomach.

To ease the distress caused by the breathing tube—and probably to ease the distress of the doctors and nurses when I spat it out—I was given a tracheotomy three days after the second neck surgery. In this operation, they cut a hole in the neck in the gap in the middle of the collar bone. The breathing tube was inserted there, straight into the windpipe. This relieved the throat and mouth irritation that had been upsetting me.

To test whether I was ready to handle solid food I had to swallow a small amount of blue dye. If they could recover any coloured liquid afterward through a suction tube that reached into my lungs then I had failed. The first few times some of the dye went down the wrong way.

To give me an incentive, the medical staff promised to give me a thickshake if I passed the test. A thickshake! A sweet, gooey, creamy, icy-cold thickshake. Real food. That was a *big* incentive. I had to find a way to beat the blue dye test.

Fortunately another patient gave me the tip: if you gulp the dye down it goes straight to your stomach. The gulp technique worked, but for some reason I didn't get my promised reward until Dad went and bought it for me. And what a disappointment. My taste buds must have forgotten as much as my muscles. The thickshake was awful.

A week after the second operation I began having short spells off the ventilator. The first time was very scary. I was only off it for ten minutes but by the end I was exhausted. I began to get dizzy. I was terrified I wouldn't be able to keep going and I was so relieved when the ventilator took over again.

Gradually I built up my lung capacity until I was having 30 minutes on the ventilator, 30 minutes off.

My physiotherapist, Jacquie, monitored my progress by having me blow into a little machine that measured the strength of my breath on a dial. Each day I set myself the target of beating my previous day's score. I only failed once. I looked forward to my daily breath test. I enjoyed having a challenge and being able to compete again, even if it was only against myself.

As my scores got higher I found new ways to beat my previous mark. After I'd blown as long and hard as I could,

I'd scrunch up my abdomen to force any air down there to the top. Like rolling up an old tube of toothpaste, I found there was always a tiny bit more left if you squeezed hard enough.

The doctors were pleased with my results and so was I, but when they told me that on my last night in intensive care I'd have to go right through to the morning with no ventilator I was very nervous. The nurses could see this and put on a little tap dance performance to ease the tension.

I made Jason sit beside my bed and watch me all night. Occasionally there would be a gurgling sound from the sputum in my windpipe and I'd squeeze Jason's arm to get it suctioned out. I made it through on my own but I hardly slept a wink that night, afraid that I'd be unable to maintain normal breathing without being awake and able to concentrate on keeping my lungs up to the job.

Even when I went off the ventilator I still wasn't able to talk to Mum, Dad, Jason or Kim at first. They took it in turns to sit by my bed from early in the morning until late at night, so that whenever I was awake there was a friendly face there. In a strange way I felt sorry for them, Mum and Dad particularly. I could see from the looks on their faces that their feelings of helplessness were as bad as mine. I knew how much they loved me and that they would give anything, do anything, to make me better. But there was nothing they could do to bring my body back to life. All they could do was try to keep my spirits up and maintain a poker face when the doctors gave them another gloomy outlook about my future.

A couple of days after I left intensive care, I had a new tracheotomy device fitted that had a little red cap on it covering the hole in my throat. When the cap was on there was nowhere for the air to escape before it got to my mouth so I was able to talk. At first I was only allowed to speak for a couple of minutes at a time and my voice came out high-pitched, like a cartoon character. It was quite frustrating. I had so much to say but only a few breaths' worth of talking capacity. But I discovered 'I love you' is just as powerful said silently as out loud—it always brought a glaze to the eyes of whoever was at my bedside.

I also discovered that if I took a deep breath at the end of a talking session, I could get another few words out after the breathing tube went back down my throat. This allowed me to play a trick on one nurse. After she had fitted the collar that held the tube in place, expecting it to render me speechless, I squeaked, 'Thanks for that.' The poor girl nearly jumped out of her skin.

Kim was a tower of strength. She dropped everything to be with Mum when Dad and Jason had to go back to Tassie to look after things at home. Mum would have been lost—literally—without Kim. Sometimes Mum would go off for a cup of coffee and be so stressed out she would forget the way back to the intensive care unit. Kim would have to go and find her. Before I came off the ventilator, Kim had also been the only one who could lip-read me properly, and she translated my morphine-addled mumblings for the family.

At first the hospital only had accommodation available for Mum and Kim in the Leslie Jenner office and accommodation wing. They had single bedrooms, but Kim took her mattress into Mum's room and slept on the floor beside her so Mum always had a shoulder to cry on.

Now that I was able to think straight, I was getting a better idea of how badly damaged my spine was. The doctors certainly didn't offer any optimism. Although I was getting better feeling in my legs they stressed that getting back movement, let alone walking, was another thing altogether.

I was trying to stay positive, for myself and the family, but there was absolutely no encouragement from the hospital staff. One young idiot doctor even said it would have been better if I had suffered brain damage—at least then I wouldn't know about being a quadriplegic.

I distinctly felt the lack of hope from the medicos at the time and it's confirmed in the hospital notes I've obtained to help with this book. Three days before I was ready to leave intensive care, the social worker's report says: 'Bev states she will recover totally and the family do not contradict her . . . Denial can be a positive method of coping with overwhelming anxiety.'

The nurse's report the next afternoon takes a similar line: '(Wonder) whether they know the full extent of injury.' The word 'full' is underlined.

Deep down, underneath my denial, I must admit I was starting to have the same doubts as the nurse and the social worker. A couple of nights before they wrote those words, when I was still in intensive care, I was up late, unable to sleep. It occurred to me that, in more than a fortnight since the fall, I hadn't really tried to make any movements apart from the standard resistance tests on my arms and legs the nurses performed every day.

I was absolutely sick of being in hospital, sick of feeling helpless, sick of lying there like a breathing corpse. 'Bev,' I said to myself, 'anything you have put your mind to in the past you have been able to do. If you try hard enough, if you put everything into it, you can make yourself sit up and walk out of here.'

I lay there for about ten minutes, concentrating, building up to that one teeth-gritting surge that would raise my lifeless body from its tomb. When I felt I'd reached my highest level of focus, I took a deep breath and mentally heaved myself off the mattress. Nothing moved. I might as well have been back on the turf at Elwick.

I wasn't giving up that easily. 'OK, I may not be able to climb out, but if I really put everything into it surely I can throw myself off the bed.' More deep breaths, more intense concentration. Another heave, with every last drop of energy I had in me. Nothing. I was spent. I broke into an uncontrollable sobbing fit. I cried and cried until I passed off to sleep.

When Kim came in to see me the next day, I said I wanted her to take me away somewhere to die. It wouldn't be the last time I would talk about taking the easy way out, but I never got to the point of seriously considering it. That day, though, for the first time, I totally understood how a person could commit suicide.

The next time I saw my physio, Jacquie, I asked her straight out: 'Why can't I move?'

I'd been told my arms would recover limited capacity and my legs, now paralysed, might get some movement back as the swelling in the spinal cord went down. I'd been given the technical term for my condition: incomplete quadriplegia. But no one had really explained, in a simple, detailed way that I could understand, what exactly had rendered my hands and legs useless.

Finally, three weeks after my fall, Jacquie put me straight. She told me about the mechanisms of the central nervous system, comprising the brain and the spinal cord, and the messages they pass to each other. The way these messages are transmitted is amazingly complex, but the basic workings of the system goes like this: There are three main sections of the spine. The cervical spine is the neck. The thoracic spine runs from the shoulders to the abdomen. The lumbar spine is the lower back. At the bottom is the tailbone, or sacral section.

In the gap between each bone in the spine, nerves branch out from the spinal cord to activate different muscles. There are seven vertebrae in the neck. They are numbered from the top: C1, C2, C3 etc. The worst damage to my cord was between C5 and C6, the fifth and sixth vertebrae. Although the burst disc had crushed the cord it had not pierced it, which is why I still had some feeling in my lower body. When there is still some feeling and movement below the level of the injury, it's called partial, or incomplete, quadriplegia. For me, this essentially meant I had some feeling in my arms and legs. When the spinal cord is completely cut there is no feeling and, most specialists say, no possibility of recovering movement below that point. That's called complete quadriplegia.

The higher in the neck the injury occurs, the greater the loss of function. Christopher Reeve, the actor best known as 'Superman', is an incomplete quadriplegic at C2 as a result of falling off a horse during a cross-country jumping event three years before my accident. He needs mechanical assistance with his breathing and can barely move a muscle below his neck by himself.

The conventional medical wisdom has been that some message transmission cells are so specialised that once they are destroyed they cannot be replaced. New research, some of it sponsored by Christopher Reeve's personal fundraising foundation, suggests stem cells and other cutting edge technologies may one day make it possible to repair even the most sophisticated spinal communication systems.

I still had some movement in my arms because my brain's messages were still able to reach the nerves above C5 and C6. The nerves at C3 go down to the diaphragm. They were still working, which is why I was able to breathe for myself. The nerves at C4 come out to the deltoid muscles and biceps at the top of the arms. They were still intact. That was why I could raise my upper arms. The forearms are controlled from C6, the triceps from C7, and the hands from the nerves below that, which is why I had no control below the elbows. The leg muscles are driven by nerves in the bottom section of the back, or lumbar spine. These nerves were blocked off from my brain by the damage at C5 and C6. The nerves that control the bladder, bowels and sex organs are at the tailbone and they were also getting virtually no signal.

The force of the blow when I hit the ground and the whiplash straight afterwards had caused my spinal cord to swell up, squashing the transmission wires used by the message-carrying cells that survived the impact. As the swelling went down some of these channels would re-open, but important wiring was destroyed when the disc crushed the cord.

Jacquie said that if I was going to get movement back it should have happened by now. The statistics showed that about one in twenty people with my type of injury got significant movement back in their legs. One in 50 might be able to get around on crutches. The odds of my walking normally again? Write your own ticket.

Spelling out the cold, hard facts was as tough on Jacquie as it was for me—by the end of her lesson we were both sniffing away tears.

The day before I left intensive care I was allowed out of the unit so Dad and Jason could take me over to see the ward I would be moving to, which was in the building next door. We were told to look in on the gym there because soon I would begin rehabilitation work.

When we got outside it was as if a spell had been lifted. In intensive care, with the 24-hour lights, the high-tech equipment and the electronically controlled temperature—always between 20 and 22 degrees Celsius—I could suspend belief that this was really my life. It was all too unnatural to be true. Outside, with the chill wind on my face, there was no denying this was the real world. When the other people in wheelchairs looked at me out here they saw the same thing I did when I looked at them: a quadriplegic.

The visit to the gym only made it worse. Around the room people were toiling away trying to build up the lost movement in their limbs. One girl was sitting on a table swinging her legs, below the knees, from side to side. It hit me right between the eyes that this was something I couldn't do, something maybe I'd never be able to do again. 'Get me out of here,' I said to Dad. I bawled all the way back to my bed.

For the first time I had begun to feel sorry for myself. In the big casino of life I'd been a steady winner. I'd built up a healthy pile of valuable chips—career, husband, family and friends. Out of nowhere a big black arm had come down and swept them all off the table. For the first time I started to ask, 'Why me?' I started to think of a life without legs, a life without riding. What sort of life would that be?

People who suffer a traumatic loss typically go through four stages of grief: denial, anger, depression, acceptance. That girl swinging her legs in the gym shook me out of denial. But I was still a long way short of acceptance. That left me stuck in the middle—confused, angry, and starting to doubt whether life in this condition would be worth living.

PART II

BEFORE THE FALL

Ted and Joan

The theory behind breeding racehorses is that by adding the genes of a champion stallion to those of your mare, you can produce an offspring that will be better than its mother. For instance, if your mare has a speed pedigree, and you want a youngster that burns the turf, you double up on go-fast genes by choosing a sire that has won elite sprint races like Flemington's Lightning Stakes or Newmarket Handicap.

Followers of this theory would say that the secret ingredient behind the success of Sunline, Australasia's champion horse of recent years, is that both her mother and father carry the genes of the North American super-sire, Northern Dancer. A double dose of speed and class.

In human terms, if you wanted a daughter bred to overcome adversity, you couldn't do much better than bring together my parents, Ted and Joan Buckingham. A double dose of battling through life's hard knocks.

My mother was given up for adoption as a baby. She didn't discover this herself until she was fifteen, when a girl from her school cruelly blurted out her secret in the middle of the street in the small English town where she was brought up.

Mum's natural father was an American World War Two soldier serving in England in 1944. In those days, working class single mothers in provincial England didn't have much choice but to give up their babies. At least Mum's pedigree didn't stand out as obviously as a number of other local children, who had been fathered by black American servicemen.

Mum's adoptive father, Henry Voss, was a dental technician in Diss, about half-way between Ipswich and Norwich in the county of Norfolk. He did his best to provide her with a good upbringing, but they never bonded as closely as Mum and Henry's wife, Frances Voss. They were as close as any natural mother and child.

Dad never knew his father either. Leading Seaman Frederick Buckingham was killed in the war when Dad was just two months old. Frederick's destroyer, HMS *Martin*, was sunk by a German U-boat. Dad's mother, Dorothy Buckingham, or Betty as she was known, added 'Martin' as Ted's middle name in honour of the father her little boy would never know.

Betty Buckingham brought up Dad, his three brothers and one sister on a war widow's pension in Stonham Aspel, a farming village of around 200 people in the East Anglian county of Suffolk, about 20 kilometres from Diss.

The six of them lived in a rented cottage on the farm of a family for whom Betty Buckingham worked as a housekeeper. Although Dad's family was poor, he loved life on the farm surrounded by rolling paddocks filled with cattle, sheep and grain crops. In those days the heavy work of ploughing the fields and harvesting the wheat and barley still relied on horses. As a young lad, Dad loved nothing more than to climb up onto one of the draught horses and let it do a bit of overtime giving him a ride.

Because his father died serving in the war, Dad was able to take a scholarship to a good boarding school, the Royal Hospital School, when he turned eleven. He did well, passing his final exams with scores high enough to gain entry to the navy college at Dartmouth.

But at the age of sixteen he had to leave his studies to go out to work and help his mother in providing for the family. He began a five-year bricklaying apprenticeship—as he puts it, this allowed the family to buy butter occasionally instead of margarine.

As well as shouldering responsibility, joining the workforce as a teenager brought Dad a bit of freedom. With the few shillings left over after his contribution to the family budget, Dad would go to dances at neighbouring village halls with a bunch of mates on the lookout for girls.

That's how Mum and Dad met. Mum had gone to a village hall to see a band. Ted asked her to dance but Mum, in her forthright style, told him to 'get lost'.

Six months later, Mum and a friend were sitting in a cafe in Diss. In came Ted and his younger brother. This time Ted directed his pick-up lines at Mum's friend and his brother flirted with Joan. The four agreed to go out on a double date. When the big night came, it didn't take long before Ted and Joan were eyeing each other off. Since that night almost 40 years ago, Dad and Mum, Ted and Joan, have been inseparable.

The wedding bells didn't ring for another twelve months, but Dad agrees he knew they were going to be life-long soulmates well before that.

Dad was 22 on his wedding day and, having completed his apprenticeship the year before, had started working for himself. Bricklayers were not in constant demand in small-town England in the early 1960s, and with Mum falling pregnant with me straight away, the newlyweds moved in with Mum's family.

I came along on 15 March 1965, a bonny little three-and-a-half kilogram girl who, Mum says, gave her no trouble with the birth.

It is interesting to wonder how my life would have turned out if my grandmother had not died from pneumonia the following year. Maybe I would have worked for Dad as a bricklayer. Perhaps I would have gravitated towards working with animals—a vet's assistant, possibly. But we would never have had the opportunity to buy a spread of land and train racehorses for their wealthy owners. The English class system just didn't make that possible.

Joan was devastated by her mother's death in September 1966. From the day after the funeral she wanted to move away from Diss to make a new start. She got into Dad's ear about emigrating to Australia. He ordered some Australian newspapers to look up such things as house and car prices. One advertisement in particular stuck out: 'Bricklayers Wanted'.

Within six months Ted, Joan and their two-year-old bundle of joy were bound for Western Australia, half the world and a whole new way of life away. Just like Mum and Dad's first meeting, our voyage into the unknown got off to an inauspicious beginning. The Australian immigration authorities booked our flight for 1 April 1967 and when we touched down at Perth airport in the pitch black of midnight, Mum certainly felt as if she was in the middle of an awful April Fool's prank. We were put on a bus to a migrant hostel near Fremantle. There was nothing picture-postcard about the view from the bus window, just blank, dark emptiness.

It was all too much for Mum, already frazzled by nervous exhaustion brought on by leaving the only place she had ever called home. Almost in tears, she didn't dare say out loud the words running over and over through her head: 'What have we done?'

In the bright, polished-glass light of morning, things looked a lot better. Mum and Dad took me on a walk through the gum trees towards the Swan River, soaking up the unfamiliar earth tones of the landscape and the vast, cobalt-blue umbrella of the Western Australian sky—even Mum had to agree it was beautiful.

When we got back to the hostel, a bricklaying contractor turned up looking to see if there was anyone willing to start work the next day. He was offering at least a month's work at top rates of pay, but there was one catch. The job, building a house on a farm station, was more than 600 kilometres away. The building crew would only be allowed one trip back to Perth every fortnight.

Mum and Dad talked about it overnight and came up with a compromise: Dad could go as long as he made the contractor find Mum and me accommodation in Perth. The contractor offered to let Mum and me stay at his house with his wife, so the deal was done. Dad set off on an adventure into the outback while Mum and I entered 1960s Australian suburbia.

It certainly beat the hostel, but Mum still felt a little uncomfortable at the contractor's house in Bayswater. The rows of characterless brick or fibro homes on their quarter-acre blocks lacked the charm of the generations-old Tudor, Georgian and Victorian cottages of Diss. And, despite the friendliness of the contractor's wife, Mum, who had only ever lived in her family home, felt a bit like an intruder.

Dad was pleased to discover bricklaying on out of town jobs paid huge money by English standards. With hardly any opportunity to spend their wages, the contractor's crew returned to Perth with a handsome bounty. It was enough to put down a deposit on a block of land in Bayswater on which we could start building a house of our own. The land of opportunity was beginning to live up to its promise.

Mum says I was an angel of a little girl to look after, but life always seemed to give her a kick in the teeth just as things seemed to be going her way. One night she had to be rushed to hospital with acute appendicitis. The appendix had burst, damaging her fallopian tubes so badly that I was destined to be an only child.

We lived in the new house in Bayswater for about eighteen months but Mum could not get used to having neighbours just a paling fence away on either side, behind us, and then another row of them right across the street. After the privacy of living down a cobbled lane in Diss, with its population of just a few thousand, she felt both hemmed-in and exposed in the suburbs of Perth.

Dad, with more work than he could handle, coped better. On top of his brickie's wages he earned good money playing professional soccer in winter. He was paid $20 a match and $5 a goal. In 90 minutes on a Saturday afternoon he could pick up another half a week's pay.

In summer Dad played tennis at the local club. When my parents hired a babysitter so they could go to a tennis club function I'd kick up a huge stink. Even then I sensed somehow that, having left our extended family behind in Britain, from now on I only had the Buckingham trifecta to bank on: Mum, Dad and me.

On Sundays we would go for drives into the Perth hinterland, sinking back into our seats as we relaxed in the wide, open spaces and peaceful country air that seemed so far away in surburban Bayswater.

On one of our drives Mum and Dad discovered a little settlement called Glen Forest. They instantly fell in love with it. The blocks were large and screened off by trees. The locals were laid back and a little quirky, people who did their own thing rather than try to be like everyone else, as the rites of suburbia demanded. In other words, they were a bit like English villagers, except with Aussie accents. When a large block with a fibro house on it came on the market, Mum and Dad snapped it up.

When we moved to Glen Forest, with plenty of land to ourselves, Dad had room to accommodate his choice of recreational animal: horses. We already had quite a menagerie: dogs, cats, birds—even a couple of joey kangaroos we raised until they were big enough to bounce off into the bush.

From a classified ad in the paper, Dad selected a seven-year-old thoroughbred named Dream Valley. What the owner didn't mention was that the mare was pregnant. Six months later I first experienced the wonder of a foal being born right in front of my gaping eyes.

Dad also bought a brumby pony, thinking it might provide me with an introduction to riding, but he was too temperamental for a five-year-old girl. Instead, I made my riding debut one hot afternoon when Dad arrived at the Glen Forest school gate sitting proudly bareback on Dream Valley. I'll never forget how special I felt being hoisted into his lap, my school chums watching jealously as Dad wheeled the big brown mare around to sashay off up the dirt road home.

This became a regular treat, especially in summer. It would get so hot—40 degrees Celsius before noon some days—that Dad would set off for work at 5 a.m. to get in a full day before the heat became unbearable. That got him home in time to be my horse-borne chauffeur. Here was the beginning of the other Buckingham trifecta: Dad, me and thoroughbreds.

The good times at Glen Forest lasted for about a year. In 1970 the Western Australian economy took a dive and the unending flow of work Dad had enjoyed began to dry up.

Reluctantly, Mum and Dad decided to look for greener pastures in the eastern States. Dad thought Queensland offered the best prospects, but Mum wanted to see if the rave reports she had heard about the rugged beauty of Tasmania and the homely charm of its people were all they were cracked up to be. The island state was always spoken of as the most English part of Australia, with familiar-sounding place names like Devonport, Swansea and New Norfolk.

As usual, Mum and Dad found a happy compromise; go to Tasmania for a look—a sort of working holiday—but if there was nothing beyond sightseeing on offer, it would be onwards up north. They sold the Glen Forest property, put our furniture in storage and found good homes for Dream Valley and all the animals except the dogs, with which Mum would never part.

I suppose we must have looked like something out of 'The Beverly Hillbillies' as we hit the road across the Nullarbor Plain loaded down with our worldly possessions, including the dogs, who were crammed in the back with me.

On our first night in Tasmania we slept in the car in the Hobart Domain. The next night we moved upmarket, to a caravan park in Glenorchy, on the west bank of the Derwent River just north of Hobart, the State capital.

Once again, the gamble of striking out on a new frontier paid off. Dad hit the jackpot straight away—six months' work for a company with a big construction job at the harbourside Wrest Point site in Hobart, building Australia's first real casino.

After the casino job finished, and with his bank balance topped up, Dad decided to go into business for himself.

He had steady work building houses, and within a few months we had gone from the caravan park to a rugged, rural property in Collinsvale, in the mountains above Hobart.

Dad bought some cows, which he would milk in the morning. Mum even tried her hand at making butter. This was the country-style life they loved.

Dad searched the 'livestock for sale' columns for another thoroughbred mare to be his farm hack, hoping he would find one that would bring the family as much pleasure as Dream Valley had.

He ended up with a mare called Emancipated, which was in foal. The night she foaled down her little filly, Dad came to wake me up for the birth. I watched spellbound as the newborn filly skittered around on her spindly legs in that magic moment when a baby horse takes its first instinctive steps.

Witnessing the birth of foals gave us all such a great thrill that Mum and Dad became more and more keen on breeding horses of their own. Dad decided to buy another mare, one with a bit of quality in its pedigree, which might produce a decent racehorse.

Teragarm, the jet-black, New Zealand-bred mare he settled on, was a good looker, but it was the lambish foal she had at her side that sealed the deal. It was a pretty expensive buy at $1500 for the pair, but Dad just couldn't take his eyes off the cute little colt.

Dad had no formal training in horsemanship but he must have had a good natural eye for horseflesh. Teragarm would go on to have six foals for us, four of them winners. And that first gentle colt, who would race as Brigadoon Boy, turned out to be a tiger on the racetrack, as good at his peak as any horse in Tasmania.

With a bit of luck he might have made himself a name on the mainland, too, but what he achieved in Tassie was more than enough. Brigadoon Boy won sixteen races and more than $30 000 in prizemoney but his significance in our family history really comes from match-making us to the racing industry—an affair that continues passionately today. Racing might have wrecked my body, but nothing else stirs my heart enough to get my rickety frame out of bed before dawn each morning to go to the track with Dad to work our horses. It's in my genes.

Dad never really intended to be a racehorse trainer.

Before he bought Teragarm and her three-week-old foal in 1973 he asked a breeding consultant for an opinion. Teragarm had only won one race and the expert said Dad shouldn't expect Brigadoon Boy to do much better.

Teragarm's family came from a long line of dour New Zealand stayers and steeplechasers. Distance horses take several years to reach their peak. The breeding guru reckoned that if Dad was hoping for racetrack glory in Australia, where the most sought after bloodlines are those of speed freaks that produce two-year-olds for the mad dash sprint of the Golden Slipper, he was wasting his time.

Perhaps the expert knew best, but in his heart Dad had already fallen for the twelve-year-old mare and her little son by the obscure Tasmanian sire, Rocky Boy.

After a few months at Collinsvale, Dad started looking around for a stud to send Teragarm to for the next breeding season. That search produced the second piece of fate that sealed the Buckinghams' betrothal to racing.

Walter McShane, a self-taught trainer born and bred in Tasmania, was running a stud farm at Broadmarsh, about 25 minutes' drive from Collinsvale. One of the stallions he stood was the English-bred Panama Mail, which had made a promising start to its stud career on the mainland.

Dad and Walter developed a quick rapport as they talked about breeding, racing and life in general. As Mum and Dad got to know the McShanes better, they would often pop in for a cup of tea and the conversation usually found its way back to horses.

Teragarm had her date with Panama Mail that spring, producing a half-sister to Brigadoon Boy that Dad named Sweet Martia. He wanted to incorporate something of his father's memory in his adventure into horse racing, but he couldn't call a filly 'Martin'. 'Martia' was the closest variation he could come up with.

By this time Brigadoon Boy was almost two years old, the age when an owner starts dreaming that the bundle of energy tearing around its paddock might be a superstar in waiting. Dad asked Walter to recommend a trainer, to which Walter, whose home-grown training methods had produced a stream of winners, replied: 'Why don't you train him yourself?'

At first Dad didn't entertain the idea very seriously. After inspecting a few trainers' stables in Hobart, though, he had second thoughts. Being in a city stable would mean Brigadoon

Boy would spend most of his time cooped up in a box of a few square metres with his stablemate neighbours lined up on either side. No privacy, no peace and quiet. That was no way for a horse (or a person) to live.

Dad applied for an owner-trainer's licence but was rejected as not having enough experience. He borrowed some books from Walter McShane about caring for thoroughbreds. He bought others about training theories. Putting this together with the knowledge about fitness he had picked up from his soccer career, he figured he might be able to train Brigadoon Boy after all.

He started going to the races with Walter when the McShanes had horses running. Six months after his initial knock-back, the Tasmanian stewards granted Dad his licence.

Unfortunately, the Collinsvale property wasn't going to be suitable for training gallopers as it had no decent stretches of flat land, so we shifted to a spread of much flatter land at Old Beach, about 20 kilometres north of Hobart.

Being an only child, I spent more time with my parents than with other children. I was never one to sit about watching television. I'd much rather be out running around, grooming the horses or helping Dad with his chores. I must have been more of a nuisance than assistance sometimes, but he would always find something for me to do. By the time I was nine or ten I had taken on his work ethic, which was to get stuck in and get things done, even if the task was more than a one-man job. Mum used to say I was 'Ted's shadow', always wanting to help with whatever he was doing around our property.

Although he was still working full-time as a bricklayer, Dad set about building a two-box stable at the Old Beach property in his spare time.

One day I saw him wrestling wheelbarrow loads of concrete blocks across to where he was building his stables and I just had to roll up my sleeves and muck in. I ran to the pile of blocks, grabbed the first one I could reach and hauled it along behind him. 'I'm not much use,' I thought, as I slid the lonely block up next to Dad's stockpile. 'He's taking a whole wheelbarrow full and I'm only carrying one.'

Dad must have read my mind. 'Every single one helps,' he said.

I went back and picked up two blocks. It took all my strength, but I was determined not to stop until we were finished. I went back for two more blocks, then two more, and two more . . . by the end, I couldn't have lifted another block off the ground.

I was proud I'd helped Dad get the job done, but a few hours later my arms still ached and my abdomen was causing me pain. By the evening I was in so much pain Mum was terrified I had appendicitis. She whisked me off to hospital, where the doctors informed her I had torn my stomach muscles!

Based on his soccer experience, Dad thought it would take about ten weeks to get Brigadoon Boy fit for racing. He took the young fellow for jogs around the roads near our property to build up his stamina, then started sharpening him up with sprints on the track a couple of days a week.

Being 'Ted's shadow' meant getting up before dawn to accompany him to the track for Brigadoon Boy's serious gallops. The experience of early morning trackwork was like something out of *Alice in Wonderland* to me. It made my heart race, watching the jockeys float along, balanced perfectly still, as the snorting beasts pounded the turf beneath them. For a little girl who loved horses, the drumbeat of galloping hooves was a siren's song that, within a year, wouldn't leave my head.

Dad would be the first to admit that it took him a while to learn what training horses for racetrack competition was all about. Brigadoon Boy's first start, on an energy-sapping soft track at the Elwick course in Hobart, taught him a big lesson.

He thought our little pet looked terrific, a glowing picture of health. To a more experienced eye, Brigadoon Boy would have looked 'soft' or 'pretty' in condition. The smooth coat of flesh that covered his ribs was evidence that the slow sessions around our roads at home were no substitute for the stamina-building slog of the training track. It also hinted that Dad's feed mix provided too much shine on the body and not enough petrol to the engine.

For the son of a steeplechasing family, Brigadoon Boy showed plenty of dash, though. He jumped to the front, putting Dad's heart in his mouth as his charge led the pack to the half-way mark. Then the pressure went on. Brigadoon Boy's fitter rivals picked up the pace, leaving our pride and joy eating clods of mud as he puffed his way down the straight. He came in last.

'Pathetic,' said Dad, more in reference to himself than the horse. A couple of weeks later, Dad gave Brigadoon Boy another start with only a slightly improved result: second last. The poor horse obviously wasn't fit enough for this sort of competition, so Dad sent him for a rest in the paddock while he reviewed his training methods.

As well as a new feed mix, he decided to change the balance of Brigadoon Boy's training schedule: more hard work at the track and just a couple of days jogging the roads around home.

By the time Brigadoon Boy came back for his three-year-old campaign, I was eleven and the thrum of galloping hoofbeats had tattooed itself on my brain.

Dad had bought me a little part-standardbred mare to take to the pony club across the road from our house at Old Beach. The club was run by Sean and Valerie Fisher. Val had ridden as a jockey in India and competed in ladies-only races in Tasmania. I became good friends with Val's daughter, Tara. We would spend hours together brushing our ponies and Brigadoon Boy.

If I wasn't already destined to be a jockey, then learning to ride under Val was the clincher. She told me about competing in the female riders' races on the sub-continent and showed me how to ride in the traditional pony club style: bum in the saddle, straight back, feet gently resting on the irons at the end of long stirrups. She also taught me the jockey's crouch: standing up in the irons on short stirrups, head forward over the horse's wither like a motorcycle rider leaning over the handlebars. I knew which pose I wanted to strike. I would gallop that pony as hard as I could as often as I could.

Even though I took a few tumbles, I never felt frightened. They say it takes seven falls before you become a proper horse rider. On that score it didn't take me too long to become a fully fledged horsewoman. As the saying goes, you've just got to get straight back on the horse to get rid of your fear. Mum says that when she was a kid she fell off a horse but wasn't game to remount. She hasn't been in a saddle since.

Between Val Fisher's encouragement, Dad's experiment with Brigadoon Boy and Mum's support, my desire to be a jockey got stronger and stronger. By the time I turned twelve I had set my heart set on it. I would even hop on the scales every now and then to see how much my weight was increasing. I think the first time I got on I was 33 kilos.

I'd always done pretty well at school, getting my fair share of As and Bs. I loved reading and the way books could take you into another world. I devoured everything from Enid Blyton's *Famous Five* and *Secret Seven* to *Star Trek* and of course, *The Silver Brumby* series starring Thowra, king of the brumbies.

But as I approached my teenage years, I was much keener on trackwork than homework. This became a bit of a problem when I started falling asleep in class because I'd been up since 5.30 a.m. helping Dad.

I think my maths teacher realised I was a lost cause when she started to give me a lecture about the importance of learning how to calculate percentages. My reply: 'All I have to know is that a jockey gets 5 per cent of the winner's prizemoney.'

Horse sense

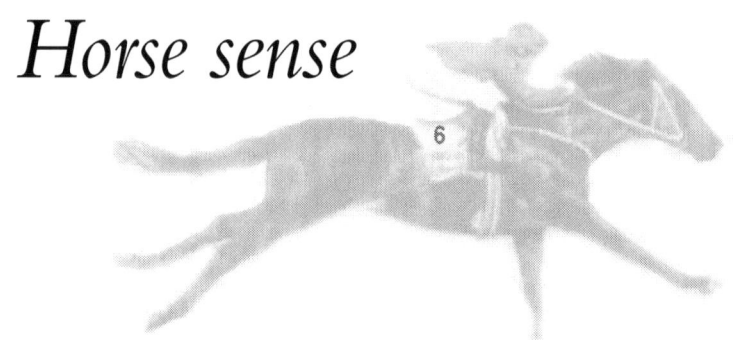

6

Dad says that from the day he first rode me home from school on Dream Valley, he could tell I had a natural affinity with horses. In more than 30 years of working with them since then, I'm still yet to meet one I really disliked.

Those lifts home from primary school, tucked safely in Dad's lap, were a wonderful introduction to horse riding. They made me feel like a little princess.

But for an unforgettable thrill, the languid walks home from school had nothing on the day Dad and Dream Valley took me on my first full gallop. Dad had cleared a 400-metre track on a gentle slope on the property at Glen Forest to see what the old girl could do. She might not have starred at Flemington or Randwick, but according to Dad's stop-watch Dream Valley could sustain a race-pace sprint on his track. That was formula one speed for the little five-year-old girl on her back. The wind rushing through my hair, the surging rhythm of the big mare's stride, the adrenaline rush of danger-level speed . . . I had been given my first fix, and I was hooked.

After we moved to Tasmania, I fed my horse habit at pony club and by following in Dad's shadow as he felt his way training Brigadoon Boy.

When Brigadoon Boy started racing, I was too young to be his official strapper, the one who led him around the race-course parade ring in front of the punters before his race. I was dying to be able to do this, and not just for the $10 the jockeys used to sling the strapper if they won. Brigadoon Boy was a family pet as well as our stable's flagship. Before his official racecourse strapper took over, I was the one who led him on and off his float, brushed him nose to tail, and whispered encouragement in his ear.

Although the gallop on Dream Valley had given me a taste of the buzz of thoroughbred racing, I wasn't prepared for the high of winning a real race.

When Brigadoon Boy came back for his second racing campaign, Dad's new feeding and training recipes made a difference straight away. Brigadoon Boy quickly showed his true ability, running second a couple of times, in each case beaten by a horse that went on to better things.

So when Dad and I set out in the back of Walter McShane's car for the four-hour drive to the meeting at Launceston's Mowbray track in November 1976, we were tense and excited.

Brigadoon Boy was in the first race, a small field of poor performers except for Brigadoon, who was a clear favourite with the bookies.

I watched Dad in the mounting yard, giving instructions to our jockey, Brian Pulbrook. I was thinking, 'One day that's going to be me.'

I remember holding Dad's hand as we took our place in the old wooden grandstand just before the starting gates crashed open. Brigadoon Boy jumped out well, settling perfectly just behind the leaders. Coming to the home turn, the commentator's voice jumped into a higher gear as the leader burst away from the field. For a moment I thought we were going to go home again with only second prize. But Brian Pulbrook quickly saw the danger, pulling Brigadoon Boy out into the clear to set off after the tearaway. Dad and I both started screaming: 'Go Brigadoon, go boy!' Half-way down the straight the front-runner began to tire. Our boy was just winding up. He sailed on by, clearing away to win by nearly four lengths.

By the time Brigadoon Boy passed the finishing post Dad was going crazy, jumping up and down, whooping like he'd won Tattslotto. He picked me up in a big bear hug. We went into a whirl, kissing and hugging and punching the air.

Dad would later say, full of irony, that that day was the ruin of him. Bricklaying might have been the business he knew backwards and could rely on to pay the bills, but no one ever danced a jig on a building site like we did in that grandstand—at least not while they were sober.

You could say it was the ruin of me, too. From that day on I lived and breathed racing, chasing that winning rush.

I never really had to come out and say to Mum and Dad, 'I want to be a jockey.' It was just something we all understood.

By the time Brigadoon Boy won his first race, when I was eleven, I had ridden plenty of slow trackwork for Dad at the Elwick track in Hobart. I would watch the senior jockeys, especially Brian Pulbrook, who took Brigadoon Boy on his fast training gallops. He always gave me helpful tips when I asked about the finer points of riding, like how to hold back a horse that just wanted to tear off around the track to get its work over and done with.

He also taught me how to keep an accurate pace 'clock' in my head. When horses are still in the basic fitness stage of their preparation, trainers like them to go at what is called 'even time', or 15 seconds per furlong (200 metres). When the horse is getting closer to race day, trainers want it picking up towards top speed at the finish of the gallop, about 12 seconds to the furlong. That is 60 kilometres an hour, but unfortunately horses don't have a speedo mounted between their ears. Over the last 600 metres of trackwork a couple of seconds either way can be crucial. On one hand, the horse could turn up on race day already burnt out, having left its big effort for the week at the training track. On the other hand, it might go down in a tight finish through not having had a true, lung-stretching gallop to clear out the cobwebs.

So it's pretty important to have an accurate 'clock' in your head. The basic technique is to count like this as you pass each 200-metre marker: 'One, cat and dog; two, cat and dog; three, cat and dog . . . ' Some jockeys have a natural instinct for it and can feel how fast their mount is going. Others have to work and work to get it right by checking their 200-metre counts against the stopwatch after every track gallop.

I was in the latter category. Brian Pulbrook would let me ride a horse alongside him to help me learn to judge the right pace. Pat Allen, another senior jockey, was also generous with his help.

Walter McShane was the first man, apart from Dad, to recognise I might have the makings of more than a trackwork rider. One morning when I was ten, Walter asked Dad if he had a horse he could trial against one of his promising three-year-olds. Walter thought his horse was ready to win. He wanted to test it against something with a bit of speed, so Dad offered to put me and Sweet Martia, Brigadoon Boy's unraced two-year-old half-sister, up against Walter's good thing.

Brian Pulbrook was on Walter's horse. I didn't go out there with the intention of proving a point, but when Sweet Martia was still alongside Walter's horse near the end of the 800-metre gallop, I let my filly have her head. When we hit the line, Sweet Martia was travelling easily three-quarters of a length in front of Walter's horse, which was being pushed along by Brian.

Walter turned to Dad and said, 'That girl of yours can ride. You might have your stable jockey there.'

At that stage, my love for horses and the fact I was riding at the track alongside the professionals made it seem perfectly sensible that, as soon as I was old enough, I would simply turn up one morning able to officially call myself an apprentice jockey.

There was only one problem. In the mid-1970s, Australian racing was still in the equal opportunity Dark Ages. Women were not allowed to ride against men, and women trainers, while not formally barred, were spotted about as often as Tasmanian tigers. It seems incredible now, with Gai Waterhouse dominating the New South Wales Trainers' Premiership and Sheila Laxon winning the 2001 Caulfield and Melbourne Cups with Ethereal, but a lady's place then was to take care of the dirty jobs and leave all the glory to the men. (That is if you don't count Wilhelmina Smith, an eccentric early 20th century jockey in country Queensland who rode as 'Bill Smith' and was only revealed to be a woman on her death in 1975.)

It wasn't until 1977 that a Victorian city race club—Moonee Valley—allowed women free access to all the areas the male members used. The Victoria Racing Club didn't do away with the notorious white line separating men and women at Flemington until 1982, and then only under pressure from John Cain's incoming Labor Government. That same year the other major Victorian club, the Victoria Amateur Turf Club, voted to do away with its white line and to allow women to become members.

In the United States, women jockeys had been accepted into the mainstream since 1969. Until 1973, the best the crusty old men who ran Australian racing could offer was an occasional lady riders' race at picnic meetings. The first city race staged for women, at Eagle Farm in Brisbane in September 1973, was won by June Lossius, a founding member of the Victorian Lady Jockeys' Association. Some of the news reports spoke of her $500 winning prizemoney as being 'handy housekeeping'.

Australia's would-be women jockeys didn't take this non-sense lying down. In Queensland, Pam O'Neill led the charge. In Victoria, Pam Baker, from Geelong, spearheaded the group that set up the Lady Jockeys' Association in 1972. After three hard years of lobbying they were given fifteen races a year at small-town tracks such as Hanging Rock, Warracknabeal and Moe.

Dianne Wynne, whose daughter Sally is one of the most successful women jockeys of the present generation, took over where Pam Baker left off. Yet it was not until January 1979 that even the progressive Moonee Valley Racing Club moved to put on the first metropolitan women riders' race in Melbourne.

The tide of the times had turned irresistibly, though. In 1977, females were granted permission to jump the risky fences of Britain's Grand National steeplechase at Aintree. The following year the rules of racing were changed in New Zealand to allow women to become fully fledged jockeys.

One of the Kiwi girls who took advantage of the changes across the Tasman was Linda Jones, the wife of a leading trainer, Alan Jones. Linda, like hundreds of other women riders around the world, had been doing all the hard yards riding trackwork while being denied the opportunity to enjoy the rewards on race day—not to mention 5 per cent of the winning cheques.

Linda had been the regular training rider of horses such as the mighty Balmerino, which, after establishing himself as an Australasian champion, went to Europe to run an unlucky second in the Continent's most prestigious distance race, the Prix de l'Arc de Triomphe. Yet the only rides she could get on a race day before officialdom saw the light were in the 'Powder Puff Derbys' put on by some clubs as novelty promotions.

Linda Jones quickly showed the New Zealand racing establishment what it had been missing out on. As well as riding regular winners, she attracted thousands of new racegoers to the track with her good looks, bright personality and ability to get the best out of her horses without punishing them.

When some of her mounts were nominated for big races in Australia, the industry chiefs knew they were in for some embarrassing publicity if they didn't follow the lead set by the New Zealanders.

On 31 March 1979, Linda Jones ended the all-male jockey era in Australia when she rode Northfleet, trained by her husband, into third place in the Manion Cup at Sydney's Rosehill course.

A few weeks later Linda went down in the history books as the first woman to ride a winner against men in Australia when she piloted Pay the Purple to victory at Doomben, in Brisbane.

It didn't take long for the home-grown girls to make their mark too. Pam O'Neill showed the boys what to expect from the keen, skilful females who had been waiting so long to strut their stuff. In May she rode three winners at one meeting at Southport, in Queensland. In Western Australia, Paula Wagg booted home a winner at her third ride.

When Linda Jones stole one of the feature races of that autumn's Adelaide Cup carnival with a daring, front-running display on Northfleet, the media joined girls like me in celebrating the fairer sex finally getting a fair go.

I was fourteen, going through the motions of grade nine at Latrobe High School, when the jockey gender barrier came down. I was so excited I couldn't wait until I turned fifteen, the official school leaving age, to start my apprenticeship. Mum and Dad sought special permission for me to leave early, which was granted in November.

When we crowded around the TV to watch Hyperno win the 1979 Melbourne Cup, I could realistically think that one day it might be me in the saddle instead of my hero, Harry White, trotting down the famous lane of Flemington roses, cheered on by the massive crowd all the way to the winner's circle.

The thing I admired most about Harry White was that he got the best out of his horse without having to bash it with the whip. You could see him thinking his way through a race so as to give his charge the smoothest possible passage— tucked in close to the rails but with room to stride out, watching all the time for a gap that would creep his horse closer to the lead with no extra effort. No wonder he still shares the record of four wins in the gruelling, 3200-metre Melbourne Cup.

I may have been the youngest female apprentice jockey in the country right then, but I wasn't the first, not even in Tasmania. Alison Anderson began her apprenticeship with trainer Larry Dalco at Deloraine just before I left school.

About a month after that, Kim Simpson (who later became Kim Dixon when she married Lenny) joined us as apprentices under her father, Cyril. Later Larry Dalco took on another girl, Tracey Warmsley.

Dad had taken on a couple of horses for outside owners and was looking seriously at becoming a full-time trainer. The opportunity to make the full transition from bricklayer to horseman came in late 1978 when Dr Michael Wilson and his wife, Sybil, who owned the Harpley Stud at Wesley Vale in north-western Tasmania, advertised for a manager. Their star stallion was the 1970 Caulfield Cup winner, Beer Street. Dad got the job.

Beer Street had the reputation of being a savage old beast, which was not helped by his nickname, 'Boozer'. I was told to keep out of his paddock for my own protection. Of course I took no notice. As I said, I never met a horse I didn't like. In the evenings I would duck under the fence to give him his bin of feed. He would dip his head in and after a few mouthfuls I had his trust. I could pat him, walk him around the paddock, anything. Within a couple of months, I could ride him bareback like an old rocking horse.

The manager's job during the breeding season gave Dad a safety net income so he could give up bricklaying while he built his new career. Our new base allowed him to take on more horses from outside owners.

Brigadoon Boy's success—he racked up a series of good wins after he broke through for his first victory—gave Dad some handy publicity. Mum saw to that. While Dad and I put in the hours with the horses, Mum had always been an important member of the team as chief publicity officer and the one who kept everything ticking over when we were off at the races.

The move from Old Beach to Wesley Vale was perfect for

us. The Spreyton racecourse at Devonport, where Beer Street and the 1972 Melbourne Cup winner, Piping Lane, had been trained, was just down the road for fast work. To give the horses a bit of variety, we could take them down to Pardoe Beach for a workout, ten minutes' drive away.

I took over riding most of the trackwork for Dad's stable, which had grown to double figures. Right from the start of my apprenticeship he drew a firm line: inside the house I was his daughter, outside I was his employee. He had learned his trade the hard way. He wanted me to learn the same discipline that had served him so well by making sure I did my share of the dirty jobs, like shovelling manure out of the horse boxes and hosing the horses down after trackwork.

It didn't worry me. If a job meant spending time with horses, I was more than happy to do it. I wasn't so pleased about having to go on a jockey's diet though. No more chocolate or ice cream!

As well as taking regular classroom lessons at the apprentice school in Launceston, I had to ride in front of the stewards in five trials before I would be allowed to take part in a real race. The first one was a breeze. Dad put me on Brigadoon Boy in a 1000-metre trial at Spreyton. Brigadoon Boy was a six-year-old by then and I knew him inside out. I just positioned him behind the lead, then shifted him away from the running rail before the home turn. He cruised home to win by two lengths. It was a wonderful feeling when we hit the lead, the same sort of thrill as that first, flat-out spree on Dream Valley.

⌒

I would have to go cold turkey for almost a year before I got the taste of a real race ride. Apprentices had to be at least fifteen to take a race mount, but even after my birthday Dad did not succumb to my constant pleading. He wanted to make sure I was ready to cope with the real thing.

Until then, Dad needed a race-day rider. He chose Leon Lucas, a young man who had been the leading apprentice in South Australia before returning home to Tasmania because of weight problems. Leon had a reputation as a bit of a wild boy, but he was a model professional at our stable.

I passed my final trial before the stewards on 5 October 1980, a couple of weeks after Alison Anderson had become the first female to ride against men in Tasmania.

Even though I was champing at the bit for my first ride, Dad didn't play favourites with me over Leon. He had two horses entered for Mowbray on 18 October, Dandy Lane and Bickley Hero. They were both having their first start in a new campaign. Bickley Hero was a handy stayer, but this old grey wasn't what he used to be in the speed department. A 1200-metre sprint was going to be far too short for him. Dandy Lane had won first-up over this distance before and was ready for a repeat performance. Dad put Leon on Dandy Lane, me on Bickley Hero.

The rest of the country's racing focus that day was the running of the Caulfield Cup in Melbourne, but for me the Wellmuir Progressive Handicap at Mowbray was the only race in town. For years all I had wanted to do was ride like a real jockey. Now here I was standing at the racecourse entrance with my new $90 saddle, riding boots, skull cap and whip, itching to mount up and canter down to the barrier, crouching low, floating across the turf like Harry White.

Unfortunately the racing club management had overlooked one small point: providing me with somewhere to get changed into my shiny new riding gear. They were still building new facilities for jockeys that would include a separate room for women. In the meantime, I was sent into the construction site to prepare for the biggest occasion of my life in a broom closet that didn't even have a working light.

It got worse from there. Bickley Hero was handicapped to carry 55 kilograms. I was given a 3-kilogram allowance as an apprentice, so I had to sit on the scales, with my saddle, at exactly 52 kilos before the race. My little 15-year-old frame came in at 48 kilos. My saddle added another 1.5 kilos. When I hopped on the scales I was 2.5 kilos under correct weight.

'Oh my God,' I thought, when I saw the needle on the scales come to rest, 'they're not going to let me ride.' Luckily, the veteran jockey Pat Allen was looking out for me. He came to the rescue with a heavier saddle with a bag for lead weights that brought me up to the right figure.

After that embarrassment, I couldn't bear to go back to the broom closet. I escaped into the mounting yard to wait for Bickley Hero's strapper to bring him out. The men had their jockeys' room to go back to, but I was left out there in front of the crowd, feeling very conspicuous, praying for the stewards' call to mount up.

It was just as well I knew my horse had no chance— I would have been a nervous wreck if I had been on the well-fancied Dandy Lane. Now I understood why Dad had put me on the slowcoach.

When I finally got legged up on Bickley Hero I felt a lot better. The race panned out pretty much as I expected. Bickley Hero settled at the back of the eight-horse field but made a bit of ground in the straight to finish second last. I was happy just to cross the line. Not as glad as Mum, who was so worried she couldn't face coming to the track, preferring to listen to the radio commentary at home.

Two weeks later I rode Bickley Hero again at Mowbray, finishing third in a four-horse field. That gave me my first 5 per cent cut of prizemoney, on top of my $26 riding fee. As an apprentice, all my earnings went into a trust fund controlled by the State racing authorities until I graduated to full jockey status.

The special thing about that day was that I also rode Brigadoon Boy in a race for the first time. I think Brigadoon Boy knew it was me aboard. He thought we were just out for a fun gallop and didn't need to observe racetrack etiquette. He certainly didn't seem to try as hard for me as he did for other jockeys. I didn't have the best of rides, finishing fourth. Afterwards the stewards noted I shifted my line three times and warned me to make sure I was clear of other horses before moving out.

Elwick traditionally holds a meeting on Melbourne Cup Day, so I only had to wait three more days for another crack at my first winner. Dad had a horse entered named Limit Man, which had won its past three starts. He was handicapped at 51 kilograms, a weight Leon Lucas couldn't get down to.

The owners, the Petropolouses, told Dad they would be happy for him to put me on, even though it would be just my fourth ride in a race. That made me very grateful, and made them part of history.

Limit Man jumped straight to the lead in the 1000-metre dash, with the odds-on favourite, War Boy, breathing down his neck. Dad had told me to hold Limit Man up for a final effort, but he hit the lead under his own steam when we turned for home. With 200 metres to go I gave him a kick in the ribs, even though we were in no danger. Limit Man romped home by nearly two lengths, taking a tick over 61 seconds to make me the first woman to ride a winner against all comers in my home State. I remember thinking, 'Well, this is a pretty easy way to make a living.'

The next day my photograph was in all the local newspapers. On the mainland, the big city dailies noted the trailblazing teenage girl jockey from Tassie.

Things just went better and better for me. In December 1980, at Spreyton, I had three rides one Saturday for a win on Dandy Lane, a second on Limit Man and a third on Brigadoon Boy.

At that early stage, some of the male riders would congratulate me after a win. Most of them seemed to think us girls wouldn't last, that we would find the going too tough once the initial thrill had worn off. There were some hard men among them, some heavy drinkers. One had such a big session the night before a meeting that when he was legged-up into the saddle for his first ride he just kept on going, landing flat on his face on the other side of the horse.

I was too wrapped up in what I was doing to worry much about what the male riders were thinking, but some of the old guard openly displayed their distaste for the new order. Max Baker, a veteran regarded as the top rider in the State, didn't say much, but he meant what he said. 'I don't really think racing is a female game, but good luck to them if they want to try,' he told *The Examiner* newspaper. He said no daughter of his would ever be a jockey.

He never gave me his thoughts directly on why women didn't belong on the racetrack. In fact, he hardly spoke a word to us girls, on or off the track.

Trainers weren't much more welcoming. When I rang Brian Lomasney, a Hobart trainer, one night to ask about riding one of his horses, he tersely replied: 'No girl will ever ride one of mine.' I was in tears before the phone was back on the hook.

To his credit, once I had proven myself with a few winners, Brian was big enough to swallow his words. Six months later he was ringing me to ask if I would ride his horses.

Guy Archer, who had a property opposite ours at Old Beach, gave me rides, but didn't make any allowance for inexperienced girls. One day at Launceston he sent me out with these riding instructions for his horse Chesapeake Bay: 'If you get beaten on this, don't bother coming back.'

During the run, I thought I'd done Guy proud by getting the horse into a handy position on the rails, but in the straight I found myself pocketed in. I knew what Guy would be saying to other trainers if I came back with a hard luck story, so I just forced my way off the fence, knocking a couple of horses outside me out of the way.

I won the race, Guy's approval and a suspension from the stewards. It wasn't the way I liked to ride—the laws against deliberately bumping other horses out of the way are there to prevent falls—but I was so determined to succeed that if I had to break the rules to prove myself, that is what I would do.

Some bookmakers were prepared to write off the girls, even when it hit them where it hurt most. Bookmaker Tony Bartlett told *The Bulletin* magazine that some of his colleagues would offer better odds on a horse I was on because they thought the male jockeys had it over me: ' . . . they take her on because she's a woman. She's costing them plenty, too!,' he said.

In that environment—of being judged inferior until you conclusively proved otherwise—it was really important to have other girls around. Alison Anderson gave it away after a few months, but Kim Simpson and I stuck on and became best mates.

Kim was almost the exact opposite of me—five-foot nothing, stocky, loud and with a fuse as short as her frame. Her father, Cyril Simpson, had been a jockey and had gone on to train. Kim left university to follow the family tradition as soon as women were allowed to ride.

From our first rides, Kim and I were very competitive, not just to show we could compete with the men but to beat each other. In our first few months she matched me winner for winner.

At first, Kim, with her stronger build and vigorous whip action, was more popular with trainers. She was also better at talking to them on their own terms, calling them by their first names whereas I always addressed them as 'Mr', as we were taught at apprentice school. Kimmy was accepted as one of the boys by the male jockeys, willing to give as good as she got with wisecracks. I was more shy and kept out of the bravado and banter.

Our different temperaments complemented each other. Kim was very quick to get fired up and there were plenty of times I had to put my arms around her and calm her down to keep her out of a fight.

For a lot of our first year, it was just Kim and I in the caravans and makeshift rooms that accommodated the female jockeys, and we became closer and closer, kicking on after Saturday meetings with the racing crowd that partied on at the Elimatta pub in Devonport.

Over the years, we have become so close that I know I can trust Kim with anything. She has been there for me in my darkest hours. That's not to say we haven't had our moments—there was a period early on when we didn't talk to each other for about a year because Kim got it into her head I had rung a trainer to try and pinch one of her rides. It was an innocent mistake—I didn't pay any attention to who rode which horse back then—but she wouldn't listen.

It got to the point where stewards would come looking for one of us in the lady jockeys' room. If they were after Kim and she wasn't there, they would say, 'Bev, can you ask Kim to come in and see us?' I would say, 'No, you'll have to ask her yourself.' Kim would do exactly the same.

It wasn't until I was involved in a fall, hitting the running rail, that Kim lifted the cone of silence. I was almost knocked out and had to be taken to the first aid room. After the race

Kim came to check on me. Since then we've been best friends.

Tracey Warmsley came on the scene on Australia Day 1981, riding a winner with her first mount. Kim and Tracey were both three years older than me and more outgoing. They were old enough to regret the restraints on their social lives of having to get up at 5 a.m. each day, but I was quite content with the company of my best friends, the horses.

By the end of my first season, in July 1981, that dedication had paid off with 22 winners. Right until the last meeting of the season, I was in with a chance of winning the apprentices' title, only one win behind Michael Micallef, who was in his second year of riding.

Dad tried to help by putting in as many runners as he could at that final meeting, but I managed to bring home only one winner from six rides. Michael also punched one home, nosing me out for the apprentices' title.

Our efforts were good enough to place him eighth and me ninth on the overall jockeys' table, still a long way behind the champion, Max Baker, with 61 wins.

It was Dad's most successful year so far, collecting 34 winners to finish fourth on the trainers' premiership.

Not bad for a self-taught former brickie and his shadow.

Queen of the Turf

7

Hope is what keeps racing—and racing people—going. Owners and trainers hope each time their mare produces a foal, or each time they buy a yearling at a sale, that it will turn out to be the next Phar Lap or Sunline, the inexpensive, humbly bred baby that becomes a champion. Those freaks of nature are just as likely to pop up in the back blocks of Hobart as the pristine pastures of the Hunter Valley. As long as you stay in the game, you've still got a hope.

Punters hope the longshot they back in the next race will be the one that covers a long run of losing bets. And every now and then the longshots do get up. At the beginning of the 1981–82 season, a bookmaker would have given you 100 to 1 or more that a sixteen-year-old Tasmanian girl named Bev Buckingham would become the first female in the world to win a State Jockeys' Premiership. Even I didn't think I had a hope. But that didn't stop it happening.

From the start of the season, in August 1981, I was on top of the jockeys' table. In racing—unlike football, where they say every win takes you closer to your next loss—every win makes the next one easier. Your confidence grows. Those split-second judgements that are the difference between a brilliant winning ride and a hard luck story begin to come naturally. You see the gaps before they appear. When you're riding like that, everyone wants you on their horse. You get to choose from the best chances in any race.

It works in reverse when you have a dry spell. No one wants an out-of-form jockey, especially trainers who think their horse is primed to win. So the more you win, the better mounts you get offered, and the easier it is to keep winning. The more losers you ride, the worse the horses you get offered, and the worse your riding looks.

When I started out no trainer, apart from Dad, would trust me with their stable stars. The experienced jockeys, in other words the men, knew the horses that couldn't run, wouldn't try or shouldn't be within kicking range of humans. Those were the ones I got to ride.

Fortunately, I didn't know these rogue horses' reputations. I just treated them like any other horse, convinced they would respond to a bit of tender, loving care. I patted them, I talked to them, I believed in them. I would tell them they were as good as Kingston Town or Manikato, the superstars of the day. And it worked. Out-of-form horses would suddenly spark up when I got aboard.

One day at Hobart I had been given a ride on an eight-year-old veteran named Storm Castle, which had a reputation as a 'dog', a horse that would not put in when the going got tough. As I walked him around behind the starting barriers I could hear the on-course broadcast of a race from Melbourne. The mighty Manikato had ground his rivals into the turf again.

I turned to Storm Castle and said, 'Stormy, you could beat Manikato, let's show 'em how good you are.' He won by eight lengths. The next week I won on him at Mowbray.

Even Max Baker and chief steward Bruce Fullerton recognised that my affection for the animal made a difference. 'She does have a special relationship with horses,' Fullerton told *Australasian Post* magazine. 'She has an uncanny ability to get the horse on her side before she even gets into the saddle.'

In the same two-page spread, Max Baker was nonplussed at how my encouraging words proved mightier than the whip. 'Would you believe she talks to them,' he was quoted as saying. 'I am still mad when I think of how we raced neck and neck to the post one day and Bev suddenly leaned over the neck of her horse and started pleading for an extra effort. I found myself suddenly half a length behind her. She just slipped that horse into overdrive and it left me beaten.'

As the longshot winners mounted up, trainers began to wake up to the fact that if I could get their second stringers home, I would be unbeatable on their top liners.

Of course, my apprentice weight allowance helped. The more a horse wins, the more weight it has to carry so that the lesser performers still have a chance. When apprentices start riding they qualify for a 3-kilogram drop off the horse's allotted weight, which is reduced as the apprentices ride more winners.

If a trainer with the best horse could put an in-form rider on, and get 3 kilos off that horse's weight handicap at the same time, he'd be prepared to overlook the fact the rider was a girl. Michael Trinder, Allan Stubbs, Graeme McCulloch and Guy Archer were four trainers who gave me chances even before that season's 'Bev bandwagon' really took off.

It helped that I had established a reputation for following a trainer's riding instructions, even when, from the stands, it looked as though I was committing tactical suicide. In my first season, Tommy Young put me on a come-from-behind horse called Piping Swallow in the Great Southern Cup, over 3000 metres. 'Don't touch the horse until 600 metres from home,' he told me.

Piping Swallow wasn't the sort of horse to do much without being asked. He dropped straight to the rear and got further and further behind. With 800 metres to go he must have been 40 lengths behind the leader, who was going at a reckless pace, but I could feel my mount had plenty left in reserve. When we reached the 600-metre marker I let the brakes off. Piping Swallow quickly reeled in the stragglers. Down the straight I weaved between tiring runners and by the time we hit the winning post we were comfortably in front.

Tommy Young, who was normally an unflappable character, admitted he had had his heart in his mouth at the 800-metre pole. The stewards told me that if I hadn't won I would have been suspended for months—holding Piping Swallow back that long might have suited the horse but it looked bad to the punters and if he'd been beaten, the officials would have had to take action to keep the public on side.

Half-way through my second season, the possibility of my beating Max Baker for the Tasmanian Champion Jockey title became the talk of Tasmanian racing.

By December the smoke signals had reached the mainland. National TV current affairs shows started flying down to film me petting the horses at home and then handling them like a professional at the track.

The high-rating 'Mike Walsh Show' flew me to Sydney for an interview to be screened across the country. As you would expect, the last thing Mike Walsh asked me on the show was for a tip at the next meeting I was riding at, which was Mowbray. The only horse I could think of that I knew I would be riding was Rhythmic Lad. He won at 4 to 1, which probably won me a few more fans.

The more success I had, the more the male jockeys started to realise that the girls weren't just a passing fad. We were becoming a real threat not only to their egos but to their livelihoods. Some of those who had been civil at the start stopped talking to me. Two notable exceptions were top riders Gary King and Craig Hanson.

No jockey expects too many favours at the business end of a race, but it is common practice, if your horse is fading well before the finish, to give a rider whose mount is full of running a bit of leeway to get past. I didn't get that professional courtesy. But when you're hot, you're hot in this business and even the cold-shoulder tactics couldn't stop my winning run.

One of the most pleasing victories for me that season was at Spreyton in January 1982 on a nine-year-old having one of his final starts. His name: Brigadoon Boy. I had ridden Brigadoon Boy plenty of times but always got the feeling he didn't take me seriously as a jockey. After all, he had known me since I was learning to ride on him as a ten-year-old novice. This day at Spreyton he was all business. As always, he sprang out of the gates, making it easy for me to find him a good position. Near the finish we were behind a wall of horses but he just bullocked his way through.

We all knew he was near the end of his career, so it was very emotional when I arrived back at the mounting yard after the race. Mum had made one of her rare trips to the track and we hugged in tears of joy. Brigadoon Boy had taught me so much; he was the first racehorse I'd ever ridden, the first horse I officially trialled on, our family's first winner . . . To ride him to victory before he retired meant so much to me.

Bruce Fullerton, the chief steward, looked at us carrying on and quipped to Dad that he expected the horse to start crying too. It was Brigadoon Boy's sixteenth and last win. It remains one of my favourite racing memories.

I copped a four-meeting suspension that month, allowing Max Baker to make ground on me. After Christmas we matched each other until one magic day in May, with twelve meetings left in the season, when I rode four winners—Limit Man, Poa Pratensis, Monsist and Gassaman—from five rides at Mowbray. After the fourth win, I was so excited I cried.

My performance led Greg Mansfield, the racing reporter for *The Examiner*, to write:

> Seldom do punters line the rails to cheer home a 12–1 winner in the last race. The reception given to Miss Buckingham and Gassaman was more befitting a Launceston Cup winner. The few remaining critics of women riders must now be silenced forever. There is no getting away from the fact that horses travel exceptionally well for Miss Buckingham . . .
>
> Three of the four winners came right around the outside of the field to win careering away from their rivals. And two of the four were not touched with the whip. Only one is prepared by Beverley's father, leading Tasmanian trainer Ted Buckingham.

That big day out at Mowbray took my season tally to 53, four clear of Max Baker. It also took me closer to the quota of wins I was allowed before losing my weight allowance. By the end of the month I could not claim a weight drop. From now on I would have to beat Max Baker on equal terms.

Dad was leading the trainers' premiership but most of his horses had come to the end of their campaigns, so I was going to have to rely on other trainers to provide me with good rides for the rest of the season.

Perhaps this was a blessing in disguise. I had turned seventeen in March and, with the natural hormonal rollercoaster of a teenage girl combining with the effects of stardom, I was beginning to give Dad some problems. I now looked forward to Saturday night disco escapades with my fellow apprentices. I had discovered boys could be more than riding rivals.

Dad would give me a Saturday curfew of midnight. When I broke it, which was too often for my own good, he would stand me down from riding the next week. It took all of Mum's special pleading powers to get me off the hook.

The winners kept rolling along until mid-June. The media hype over my looming, ground-breaking premiership win was getting harder and harder to cope with.

The pressure of holding my lead in the jockeys' table started to influence the way I rode. I would go for home too early rather than trust my natural instincts.

Then one day at Elwick, with two race days between me and the title, it all came to a head. Two mainland press photographers were in my face from the moment I left the jockeys' room, even leaning over the running rail for a close-up of me in the barrier stalls. I felt so uncomfortable it affected my concentration during my races. By the end of the day, I was so stressed out I went to Bruce Fullerton to ask if he could do something to protect me. He agreed to keep photographers away from the female jockeys' room and the weighing-in enclosure until the end of the season.

The media glare wasn't the only thing distressing me. At 1.65 metres (5 feet, 5 inches), I was quite tall for my age. As my body matured, the lightweight rides under 50 kilos became harder and harder to make. I had a real sweet tooth, so Mum made sure there were no lollies or chocolates in the house. I had to hide my occasional treats in the jockeys' rooms.

You can learn more about instant weight loss in an hour from an experienced jockey than from a whole year of watching day-time TV. It didn't take long for me to find out how to medicate my way to the right weight. Lasix is a tablet that rids your body of fluid. Jockeys call them 'piss pills'. Duromine is a drug that suppresses appetite. It was perfectly legal for jockeys to use these drugs back then, but some racing authorities have now banned diuretic drugs because of the potential danger to jockeys. Overuse can cause dizziness, high blood pressure, anxiety, irritability and even heart problems.

On Saturday nights after the races I would be washed out and starving. I'd go on a junk food binge that would put me up to 54 kilos by Tuesday. On Wednesday I would cut back to coffee for breakfast, soup for lunch and a sandwich for dinner. On Fridays I would take the Lasix and Duromine. By race one on Saturday, I could sit on the scales at 49 kilos. After the last race it was back on the binge/starve rollercoaster.

The dieting and drugs almost killed me. In mid-1984 I was driving to a meeting in Hobart for which I'd had to waste hard to make a lightweight ride. I was cruising down the highway at 100 kilometres an hour in my Mazda 626 when the pill-induced dehydration caught up with me and I began to feel woozy. My vision went blurry and before I knew it the car was snaking across the gravel at the side of the road.

'I'm dead,' I thought, as the car veered across three lanes, hit an embankment and flipped onto its roof, throwing me between the front and back seats.

I came to my senses to hear Kim Simpson, who had been driving behind me, screaming my name through my car's shattered back window. Luckily I got away with a night in hospital under observation for shock.

A lot of jockeys used Lasix on race day itself. I tried that once, but I found I couldn't handle it that close to having to control a horse at high speed. By the end of a race I would hardly have enough energy to hold onto the reins. Some jockeys would be so distressed they would lean over after the finish to vomit but their empty stomachs had nothing to bring up. It was only the body's natural 'drug', adrenaline, that would get them going again for the next race.

After my four-winner day at Mowbray in May 1982, Max Baker was suspended for four meetings. While he was out I extended my lead to ten.

By July, the last month of the season, all the media pressure, the dieting and my anxiety over the premiership race got the better of me. I went three meetings without a winner until Mowbray came to the rescue again. I had two wins from three rides there on 17 July.

Coming into the last meeting of the season, I had 63 winners, a lead of seven on Max Baker. He would have to ride every winner on the eight-race card to beat me and hold onto the title he had held for the past seven years.

He had no luck in the first. When he missed out in race two I could finally relax and enjoy my entry into the history books.

It was a shockingly cold Hobart winter's day, and despite my warm inner glow there was not much about my riding at Elwick that day to get fired up about. The best I could manage was a second and a third placing. In the race before the premiership presentation I finished last.

That was all forgotten when the chairman of the Tasmanian Racing Club, Roy Winzenberg, handed me the bronze statuette that goes with the premiership.

TV camera crews surrounded me as I made a short speech thanking Bruce Fullerton, the other jockeys, and most of all my boss. 'He's the greatest father in the world.'

The publicity machine went into overdrive for the next couple of weeks. My feat made the sports pages around the world. The first line of the next day's *Examiner* story read, 'The King is dead, long live the Queen!' The Tasmanian country and western performer Ron Shegog put out a song on the same theme, titled 'Queen of the Turf'.

Two weeks after the presentation at Elwick, we celebrated at the official racing industry awards night at Wrest Point Casino. I wore a glamourous evening dress and Dad was spruced up in a suit and tie. We'd come a long way since roughing it and sleeping in the Valiant that first night in Tasmania: in a decade, we had gone from the tradesman's entrance to the red carpet.

'Gary'

I always looked to Dad as my career role model, but he says there was one significant difference in the way we went about our business. For him, enjoying life was more important than being number one. He could have been the top trainer if he had taken on more horses than he did, but he felt a dozen was the most he could handle, given the amount of personal attention he believed in giving them. Ted made sure he had a day away from the horses each week to play golf, visit friends or just catch up with a good book or what had been going on in the world. All I focused on was looking after the horses at home and winning on them at the track. In summer I'd go swimming sometimes and twice a month I went ice skating with Kim, who had started bringing along her boyfriend, Lenny Dixon, another jockey.

I didn't have time for any other interests except reading. Duromine stops you sleeping well and I'd be up until 2 a.m.

with the latest Stephen King thriller. When I woke up, it was straight back to work.

In the afterglow of the premiership, I began to appreciate that winning doesn't automatically make you happy. There was a cartoon in the *Saturday Evening Mercury* the night I took the title showing me standing on a smiling model of planet Earth. The caption said, 'On top of the world'. Apart from moments of special personal satisfaction, like winning on Brigadoon Boy or holding up the premiership statuette for the cameras, towards the end of what appeared to be my fairytale winning season, I didn't feel on top of the world.

The side effects of the weight control drugs caused bouts of moodiness, which led to flare-ups with Mum and Dad. It wasn't that I had lost any respect for them; sometimes my body chemistry just reached the point of spontaneous combustion. Being such a close family meant they were the ones who got burnt.

One of the bonuses that came with my winning year was a trip for two to the Gold Coast, in Queensland, for having been the top jockey at Mowbray.

I thought two weeks in the Queensland sun, with none of the usual regimentation of what I could eat, what time I had to get up and what time I had to go to bed, would be all I needed to restore me to carefree happiness.

I invited Kim along and we had a ball, taking in the theme parks, scoffing ice creams and working on our suntans. We kept our weight in check by riding bicycles everywhere, but this form of transport was essentially an economy measure—Kim left her purse in the toilet at the airport when we arrived and we had to survive on $500 spending money.

The Gold Coast Turf Club asked if I would ride at their meeting while I was there. I thought about it for two seconds before turning them down. I was sick of horses, horses, horses and racing, racing, racing.

That was when I realised just how much the stressful year of living famously had affected me. It wasn't the horses' fault I was torturing my body each week with my unhealthy diet of junk food and pills. It wasn't the horses' fault reporters and TV crews had been following my every move for the past three months. I resolved to just enjoy myself and remember why I got into this business in the first place: for the love of the animals.

That was fine while Kim and I continued to hit the beach by day and discos by night. As soon as I went back to work and looked at the scales though, the pressure was back on. I could forget riding horses on the minimum weight without my little medicinal helpers.

Dad didn't have many runners in the early part of the 1982–83 season, so I got off to a slow start. By Christmas, though, I had picked up momentum to be on top of the jockeys' table.

Despite the premiership win, there were still a few die-hards whispering that my winning the title had been a fluke and that without an apprentice's weight allowance I wouldn't be able to stay at the top. I was determined to silence them. Perhaps a little too determined.

Bruce Fullerton had moved to South Australia and was replaced by Rod Brown, from the mainland, as chief steward in Tasmania in 1982–83. I think Brown was determined to stamp his authority on the top riders in his first few months. I should have realised that in a contest between an ambitious, aggressive jockey and a chief steward establishing control in his new territory there could only be one winner—the steward.

At Deloraine on 31 January 1983 I got into trouble for causing interference on Limit Man. The stewards had opened an inquiry into the race but hadn't held the hearing by the time of the next meeting, five days later at Elwick.

This was the height of the Tasmanian summer carnival, the richest and most prestigious events on our racing calendar, the Tassie equivalent of the Melbourne spring carnival. One of Dad's horses, Relko Star, was at that time one of the favourites for the Launceston Cup, the second biggest race in the state.

These rich races only come around once a year, so every jockey is trying extra hard. It's like football players when the finals arrive. Week in, week out you go out to do your best, but you can't always conjure the intensity that comes naturally when you know this is the only contest anyone will remember in years to come. For all my success, I still hadn't won one of the big cups. Neither had Dad, so for both of us this was the next frontier to conquer.

My cups carnival was one to remember, but for all the wrong reasons. That day at Elwick I got suspended early for a winning ride on Bickley Bogan. I had taken him wide on the home turn and, although we did drift in by the width of about four horses down the straight, I thought we were far enough in front that we hadn't cut anyone off. The stewards said I had inconvenienced runners inside me. Worse, I had not made any attempt to straighten my horse or stop riding him full bore. The four-meetings suspension meant I would not be able to ride Relko Star in the Launceston Cup.

By the end of the day that would be the least of my worries. In the last race I rode Bickley Bazza. Coming to the turn he was camped behind the leaders, travelling strongly. There was an opening ahead, not quite big enough to go clean through.

In these situations a jockey has two choices. You can take hold of your horse and hope the gap opens further to allow you through. If the horses in front hold their line, you're blocked and lose any chance of winning. The other option is to press on, using your horse's momentum to prise the gap open, but this carries the danger of barging into the horses in front and a suspension for careless riding. I chose to press on.

After the race I was called into the stewards room. I was told I would face a charge of foul riding for forcing my way through the gap, one of the most serious offences in the book.

Perhaps Rod Brown was trying to make a point, given that I had been suspended earlier that day and still faced a charge from five days before. Usually the charge for causing interference is careless riding—the equivalent for someone driving a car would be speeding. The equivalent of foul riding is being charged with drink driving at twice the legal limit. That was reflected in the sentence the stewards dished out when they found me guilty on the foul riding charge—suspended for eight meetings, served concurrently with the earlier four-meeting suspension.

Two days later the stewards delivered the verdict held over from Deloraine. They found me guilty. Another four-meeting suspension, to be served concurrently with the two from Elwick. The message was clear. The Queen of the Turf was not untouchable. Send her off to the tower to think about mending her ways.

Under Bruce Fullerton I didn't always agree with the stewards' decisions, but I accepted them. I couldn't accept the foul riding charge, however, and neither could Mum or Dad. We rang Bruce for some advice. He recommended we appeal, pointing out that if the foul riding offence stayed on my record I would be crossed off the invitation list to jockeys' events overseas, as well as carrying the stain of having been found to have deliberately endangered fellow riders. I appealed to the Tasmanian Racing and Gaming Commission, which downgraded the offence and my suspension to six meetings.

The stewards' scrutiny and the six-week layoff didn't dent my confidence. I arrived at Mowbray for my first meeting back, thinking, 'How many winners will I ride today, two or three?'

It would be more than two months before I found my way back to the winner's circle. It's a common phenomenon with apprentices who have extraordinary success in their first couple of years. Things happen so naturally that you start to think riding winners just comes automatically. It doesn't, as I discovered with a frustrating run of minor placings and down-the-track finishes in the weeks after I resumed riding.

I managed only five more winners in the last two months of the season, enough to win the apprentices' title but leaving me fourth overall. You don't get flown to Sydney for national

TV interviews when you finish fourth. After the high of winning the premiership the year before, it was a real let-down.

I tried to work out what had changed. There was one race that stuck in my mind. Coming to the turn, my horse had been struggling to hold its position, so I was hard at work pushing it along. Then I felt my backside hit the back of the saddle. That had been a surprise because I liked to get my weight forward to help the horse's momentum. I thought, 'What's my weight doing back there?' and immediately leaned forward. Presto! Suddenly my mount had been able to pick up his feet. Then he was travelling as well as anything in the race. We ended up winning.

Without realising it, I had lost my natural style. I had been worrying too much about what was causing my falling success rate, rather than being relaxed and letting things flow naturally.

'Gary' changed all that. 'Gary' was my pet name for Ex-directory, a younger half-brother of Relko Star.

When Dad first laid eyes on Gary, at a parade of yearlings for the 1982 Launceston sale, he dismissed him as being too small and crossed him off his list of lots to bid on. Everyone else must have done the same because Gary was passed in and sent home.

Mum liked him though. She doesn't have the technical expertise for spotting faulty knee joints or weak cannon bones like Dad has, but she can sense something in the character of a horse. When she likes one, you should pay attention—they always turn out to be winners.

So when Joan told Ted to go back and have another look at the little colt, he drove out to the stud that had failed to sell Gary at auction. They accepted Dad's offer of $2000.

From the day he was broken in, no one rode Gary but me. He was a natural, powerful athlete, but also gentle and intelligent—when I was working around the stable, I would have the radio on and whenever a race commentary came on I could see Gary tuning in with his radar-dish ears.

Even though he was a colt, he never let the pretty fillies distract him when he went to the races—he was there to do a job. Later in life he was able to make the distinction between mares wearing rugs, who were therefore in training, and those flashing their bare flesh and who were now obviously ready for a good time.

Gary showed promise from his first start, but it wasn't until the end of 1983, as a three-year-old, that he showed signs of becoming the best horse we had ever had.

In November he won the first start of his new campaign at Spreyton. As the summer carnival warmed up, Gary was just beaten at Elwick in December. This was a lead-up towards his real target, the Tasmanian Derby, a race that had given Dad his biggest win with Pass the Baton in 1981. At his next start, in January, the racing public found out how good Gary was. He thrashed Forest Gum, who had just won the Devonport Cup, in the Derby Trial.

Dad was so confident Gary would win the Derby a fortnight later he had already begun planning a Melbourne campaign for the big cups later in the year. You can never plan too far ahead in racing. A few days before the Derby,

Gary came out with a severe skin rash that meant we couldn't put a saddle on him for his vital final training gallops. With the benefit of those final workouts, I'm sure Gary would have won the Derby, rather than finishing third. It was one of those deflating things you have to learn to live with in this game.

I also had a bit of learning to do when it came to trying to play the vet. We had a special fish oil that we'd put on Gary's skin rashes. A couple of days before one big race I wanted to make sure he would have no last-minute flare-ups, so I plastered him from head to toe with this oil. The next day when Dad took him out of the box he was horrified to find Gary's system had reacted to the oil overdose by swelling all his joints and blowing up his skin in huge lumps.

Dad grabbed every bottle of shampoo he could find and washed Gary down until the last trace of oil was gone. By race day the swelling had gone down, but his coat was dry and crusty. I felt terribly guilty when I dismounted after the race—he ran third in an event he should have won—to find all the skin under his saddle strap had broken away and he'd been rubbed painfully raw.

It was another lesson that trying too hard can backfire.

I finished the 1983–84 season with 36 winners, only one more than the year before, leaving me fourth on the overall list again. Robyn Clarke had easily beaten me for the apprentices' title with 50.

While it may have looked from the outside like I was dropping back into the pack after one fluke premiership, on the inside I was feeling much better about my prospects than a year before. At the end of the 1983 season, the fall from queen to lady-in-waiting had come with such a jolt that I had begun to doubt myself. At the end of the 1984 season, my success rate had hardly improved, but I had begun to realise how much learning I had to do before my apprenticeship was complete.

Gary was teaching me some valuable lessons. He was the first horse I had ridden that you could ride as if you were driving a souped-up car. If a gap opened in front of us, I could crouch a little lower, a signal to him to change up to overdrive. Zoom! We were through the gap into a better position. Then, just as quickly, you could chop him down a gear with a tug on the reins. Set cruise control. After that it was just a matter of waiting until the other riders started to crack their whips in the home straight. Find some galloping room, let out a little more rein, press overdrive again. See you later, boys.

When you have this sort of horsepower under you, you can ride with confidence. With confidence, you make the right choices at the right time. The winners start to flow. The good mounts follow. The winning circle is complete. I knew that when Gary and I teamed up again for his next campaign, the wheel would turn.

Another reason I was not as down about not being leading rider was that I had found my first serious boyfriend, Brendon Larkins. He was a jockey, two years older than me, also based in the north-west. We started going out early in 1984.

Brendon was a happy-go-lucky character, tallish for a jockey, with light, curly hair. He was a talented rider but had heavy bones and had to take up riding in hurdles races, where the horses carry higher weights.

After we had been going out for a while, Dad hired Brendon to ride trackwork for him and he came to live on our property, sharing a room with another track rider. Having a romantic interest helped take my mind off falling down the premiership table. While riding remained the most important thing in my life, the difference between me at seventeen and nineteen was that it was not the *only* thing.

My resurgence from number two apprentice in Tasmania to the big league began to fall into place when Gary returned to the stable for the 1984–85 season.

Dad had targeted the big three Tasmanian cups—Devonport, Hobart and Launceston—for Gary's summer campaign. In early December Gary showed he was on target by winning over 1800 metres at Spreyton.

It was no coincidence that three days after this I rode three winners from three rides at Elwick. The old feeling of being at one with my mounts was coming back.

On Boxing Day I rode Gary to another easy win in his lead-up to the Devonport Cup. Two days later I chalked up another treble. On New Year's Day I booted home three from three for Dad, taking me to the lead in the jockeys' premiership.

That put me in the right frame of mind for the Devonport Cup. The Cup carried the least prizemoney of the three majors, $15 000 that year, but being our home ground cup, it carried special significance for us.

We were confident Gary was the best horse in the field—he was also the bookies' favourite—but Dad was leaving nothing to chance. When *The Examiner* newspaper asked to photograph Gary a couple of days before the race, Dad refused. There is an old superstition in racing that having your horse pictured in the paper before a big race brings bad luck.

Instead, *The Examiner* featured another favoured runner, Ensign Piper.

'He can't win it now,' I told his trainer, Barry Campbell.

As it turned out, we would need all the luck we could get. The cup was a brawl of a race from the word go, with horses being shunted and checked right through the field. Everywhere I took Gary we found trouble. With 700 metres to go we were well back and losing touch with the leading bunch. I decided to pull to the outside, away from the buffeting. From there I got a nice trail behind the horse inside me, which was running on strongly.

Turning into the straight, it seemed we would both be too late. A top quality horse like Gary doesn't think like this though. He lowered his head, stretched out his neck and willed himself on. With 100 metres to go, the leaders were wilting but Gary was in overdrive. Now it was down to us and the horse we had made our run with to fight it out. A few giant strides later Gary flashed past the post to win in track record time.

It had been such a boxing match that it wasn't until I was trotting back to the winner's enclosure that the joy of winning the biggest race of my career took hold. To win our first big cup was a major career step for Dad and me. To have done it with a horse Mum had picked out, a horse that had been my personal pet and taught me so much about being a jockey—it was the best feeling in the world.

Oh, and that horse we beat that cleared a path for us when we needed a lucky break? Ensign Piper, the one who had his picture in the paper.

Cups fever

Every kid serious about sport has their Holy Grail. For little boys playing backyard footy, it's holding up the AFL Premiership trophy or plunging over the try line to win the Rugby World Cup for the Wallabies. The kid who cleans up the sprints at Little Athletics every Saturday morning rides home in the back seat of the family Commodore picturing themselves on the Olympic dais, kissing the gold medal around their neck. For a young jockey, the dream is pumping the air with your fist at the winning post in the Caulfield and Melbourne Cups.

As much as I was thrilled at having the Devonport Cup sitting on the mantlepiece, the real buzz from that win was the prospect of taking Gary to Melbourne in the spring for a tilt at the big cups.

Three weeks into the 1985–86 season Dad, Gary and I were on a boat to the mainland. Dad had arranged to stable Gary at Flemington, the home of the Melbourne Cup, and after he settled in Dad left me in charge—he had to be at home in Tassie to keep the rest of the team going. Kim had stepped in to lend a hand riding trackwork.

As a raw twenty-year-old, it was hard to keep my mind on the job as I walked across racing's most hallowed ground to trackwork those first few mornings. Turf gods such as Bart Cummings would wander past and I would have to pinch myself. *The* Bart Cummings, the 'Cups King'. Flemington, home of the race that stops the nation. What was I doing here?

When I climbed on Gary for his first training gallop, I felt as conspicuous as if I were performing a striptease. All the old hands would be checking out this so-called wonder girl who had blown in from across Bass Strait. For the first time in my life I was embarrassed to be seen with Gary. He had this habit of throwing his head around in his working gallops, more the friskiness of a powerful stallion than bad temper. It didn't matter in the privacy of our home training tracks, but out here at fabulous Flemington all I could think of was the early morning aficionados slowly shaking their heads and saying, 'That sheila doesn't know how to handle a horse.'

Gary's first start was in the Aurie's Star Handicap at Flemington, a traditional pipe opener for potential Melbourne Cup runners.

I was much more nervous than usual before the race. In Tasmania I had earned respect as one of the top riders in the State, a big fish in a small pond. Here I was not only a small fish in a big pond, but a breed apart. In Tassie, women jockeys were just part of the scenery every Saturday—one day the previous season, four girls had combined to win six of the seven races at Spreyton. In Victoria, Therese Payne was the only girl with any profile and she was getting few city rides. I was all alone in the Flemington lady jockeys' room on Aurie's Star day.

Out on the track, things were much more intense than at home. In Tasmania there would be plenty of banter behind the barriers. Here the jockeys stayed in their own zone, concentrating, planning, pumping themselves up. Except for Greg Hall, that is. 'How's it goin' sweetheart,' he'd say if I caught his eye. That was as far as the pleasantries went out on the battle ground. As soon as the gates opened he rode as tightly as anyone else. No one gave an inch.

Gary's run in the Aurie's Star proved he was right up to the standard of the big smoke. From back in the field he powered home for fifth—the *Sporting Globe* picked him out as the horse to watch from the race.

In racing you hope for the best, expect the worst. At his next start, in the Memsie Stakes at Caulfield, Gary bowed a leg tendon, an injury that would sideline him for almost a year.

It was disappointing to have to go home without having the opportunity to pit Gary against the best in the land in the big cups, but the trip had given me the chance to see what it was like on the big stage. I knew now that this was where I wanted to perform.

With Gary out of action, Dad didn't look to have a contender for the big Tasmanian cups in the coming summer.

That was until Dark Intruder scored his third win in a row in the Show Cup at Elwick in late October. When he won again in early January 1986, he was touted as one of the leading chances for February's Hobart Cup, the 'Melbourne Cup' of Tasmania, carrying prizemoney of $60 000, the richest race in the State.

The race before the Hobart Cup was the Invitation Stakes, which featured some of the top riders from the mainland, including the Victorian wonder boy, Darren Gauci, and my hero, Harry White. I managed to win the race, which was the perfect confidence booster for the Hobart Cup.

When the pressure went on in the big race, Dark Intruder picked up the bit and charged around the field. Down the straight, he went further in front, without having to be pushed. At the post I was easing him down five lengths clear.

After the disappointment of the spring this was a terrific boost. A month before coming out of my apprenticeship I had won the State's biggest race, leaving only the Launceston Cup to complete the big three. (That would come twelve months later on Brave Trespasser. It was a special win, not only qualifying Brave Trespasser for the Caulfield Cup, but gaving me the chance to show visiting Melbourne trainers and jockeys what I could do.)

For the second year running I was the hottest thing of the summer carnival. Gary had returned from his injury and was soon back in the winner's circle. On 30 November at Mowbray he ran in the Craig Hanson Memorial Stakes, a race that meant a lot to me because of my respect for Craig, who was killed in a race fall in 1983. Craig had had integrity, both as a rider and a person. He had been one of the few to treat me like an equal—even in my early days when I copped a few suspensions for interfering with his mounts.

I had already ridden two winners on the eight-race card before Gary came out to show he had lost none of his class. When Craig's father, Ken, presented me with the trophy I couldn't help but cry. Winning on Gary in Craig's memorial race had been the focus of the day; having had a couple of other winners earlier was a nice bonus. Going home with five wins hadn't entered my head. They were nearly all close finishes but each time I got the nod. For the record, my famous five were Neat Blessing (at odds of 9 to 4), Remainder Man (9 to 1), Exdirectory (3 to 1), Braelita (7 to 2) and This Autumn (11 to 2). That day's haul rocketed me to the top of the premiership ahead of Stephen Maskiell, a former Victorian who had replaced Max Baker as my strongest rival after Max's retirement at the end of the 1984 season.

A week later it was Tasmania's turn to host the Queen's Cup, a race in honour of Queen Elizabeth II. Gary won in a canter, and I received a personal letter from the Queen, a keen follower of the 'sport of kings'. She wrote that it was especially pleasing to be able to congratulate a woman jockey on winning her race.

Gary's return to form prompted Dad to try a hit-and-run raid to Melbourne on New Year's Day 1987 for the biggest summer distance race, the Bagot Handicap. Once again it ended in tears.

Gary was travelling well until 1000 metres from home when he suddenly dropped back through the field. I didn't try to push him along, I knew something must be wrong. I could feel him faltering from a bowed tendon in his right foreleg so I pulled him up short of the winning post. As the crowd cheered home the winner, I led Gary up the home straight for the last time. I could tell he was in pain and it broke my heart to see him end his racing days like this.

The Launceston Cup, a month after the Bagot Handicap, was worth $101 000, enough to attract some of Victoria's best stayers, trainers and jockeys.

Melbourne's champion jockey, Michael Clarke, came over to ride Noble Tinjar for the wily George Hanlon, trainer of three Melbourne Cup winners. Noble Tinjar was the heavily backed favourite ahead of two other Victorian runners, Pekamagess and the topweight, Cylai. The latter was trained by Geoff Murphy, who had won the Caulfield Cup–Melbourne Cup double with Gurner's Lane in 1982. Cylai had bagged the Hobart Cup for the Victorians three weeks earlier. Murphy said he didn't see any of the locals being a threat this time either.

Our hope was Brave Trespasser, a 20 to 1 outsider. Even his owner, Greg Richardson, thought the mainlanders would be too slick for us.

In the mounting yard before the race, with 10 000 Tasmanians packed into the newly renovated Mowbray race-course, Dad and I knew we would have to come up with something special. Brave Trespasser's racing style was to sit back until the last 800 metres and then grind his way past the runners in front as their stamina was put to the test. I was worried that if we gave the classy Victorians too much of a start we'd never catch them. Dad and I agreed I would have to push Brave Trespasser up close to the lead early in the race and try to get to the front before the home turn.

The 4 kilograms extra that Noble Tinjar and Cylai had to carry might enable Brave Trespasser to hold them off.

We started from barrier three, right beside the wily ex-Kiwi Gary Willetts on Cylai. For the first half of the 2600-metre journey I sat in behind Willetts, making sure he didn't get too far in front of us. He was biding his time in behind the leading bunch, banking on being able to out-sprint them at the end. Which is why he was caught out, like all the others, when I took off 1000 metres from home. 'One of the locals just having a rush of blood,' the mainlanders probably said to themselves.

Coming to the turn, I had set up the break we had planned on. I knew then the cup was ours. Brave Trespasser always saved his best work for the finish. Pekamagess, Noble Tinjar and Cylai were chasing as hard as they could, but Brave Trespasser was just getting further in front. Half-way down the straight the mainlanders could not believe their eyes. Who was this Tasmanian nag strolling towards the finish line four-and-a-half lengths clear? The locals loved it, cheering us all the way back to the mounting yard.

That day, that ride, was the culmination of three years of gradual discovery—working out what it took to be a top professional jockey. In the first couple of years I didn't study any form guides. As long as my horse was happy, I believed it would run for me. The rest would take care of itself. That natural affinity with the horses, an apprentice's head start of carrying less weight, and the confidence that came with winning carried me to a premiership. Now, through riding top horses like Gary, Dark Intruder and Brave Trespasser in the big cups for three summers, I had added tactical knowledge to my armoury. Hands and heels were enough to win for most of the year, but against the hardened Victorian raiders, you needed to use your head as well. I had learned the lessons of my lean years.

Off the track, my horizons were also widening. Through my cups success, I became a regular on the big sports functions circuit, mixing with Tasmania's leading sporting achievers, businesspeople and politicians.

You didn't find many women at these occasions, at least not many who weren't there because they were somebody's wife. I enjoyed dressing up, feeling glamourous and feminine on these big occasions, but I didn't want to spend the night engaged in small talk about fashion or children. I preferred being part of the man's world, where life was for the taking.

I got to meet people like John Bennetto, the veteran Sydney–Hobart yachtsman and racehorse owner-breeder, and Michael Hodgman, the flamboyant lawyer, politician and racing nut. People who had money and made their own destiny. It opened my eyes to what was possible in life, and made me want to better myself. I didn't want to die wondering whether I could really match up to the best on racing's fields of dreams—Caulfield and Flemington.

Caulfield Cup Day 1987

It's dreary, wet and cold, but the punters are still packed six-deep as the horses parade for the big race. The drizzling rain is not enough to dampen the pre-race buzz, a heady mixture of tradition, tension and imminent reckoning.

It's not the finest assembly of horseflesh the 2400-metre classic has attracted, but the roll call of jockeys is a *Who's Who* of great riders of the decade.

First onto the muddied track, on Field Dancer, is Pat Hyland. He won the race three years before on Affinity, then followed up the next year by winning the Melbourne Cup in front of the royal guests, Prince Charles and Princess Diana.

Prancing out the mounting-yard gate behind him is Colour Page, ridden by the flamboyant Jim Cassidy. Only a few years into his Australian riding career after crossing over from New Zealand, Cassidy is already immortalised for his last-to-first win in the 1983 Melbourne Cup on Kiwi.

Next out is the favourite, Cossack Warrior, prepared by master trainer Colin Hayes. His stable jockey, Michael Clarke, is running hot, having set a new Victorian record of 85 winners in the season just finished.

Peter Cook pilots number five, Balciano. This controversial but gifted rider has already won two Melbourne Cups and partnered the legendary Kingston Town to two of his three Cox Plates.

Behind him, on Ima Red Man, comes Darren Gauci, the apprentice sensation who won three Victorian premierships in a row before Michael Clarke knocked him off.

Once-a-year racegoers might mistake the boyish features of Brent Thomson, on Lord Reims, for inexperience. But Thomson knows the ropes. He added the 1982 Caulfield Cup to his three Cox Plates before heading to England to ride for millionaire owner, Robert Sangster. The call of the Caulfield Cup and the Melbourne spring carnival is still strong enough to lure him half-way across the world though. He's as focused as a microscope, even though his mount is a 14 to 1 chance, not having managed to finish in the first ten in its past three races. To cap it off, he is stuck with the outside gate of the 18 runners.

Harry White is the benchmark of riding in big distance races. He has two Caulfield Cups and two Melbourne Cups under his belt as he trots number ten, the much-hyped New Zealander Secret Seal, to the starting stalls.

Thousands of eyes then flick down the race book page to number eleven, Best Time, a 33 to 1 longshot. No need to dwell there.

On to number twelve, Brave Trespasser. This plain bay is 66 to 1, the rank outsider bar one. Nevertheless he is worth a second look. He is about to go into the history books. His jockey, Beverley Buckingham, is the first woman to ride in a Caulfield Cup.

In front of more than 26 000 people, rubbing shoulders with riders I had until then idolised through the filter of a television screen, I am excited, proud and a little bit intimidated at being part of Australia's second most famous race.

And until the morning of the race, I thought I had a real chance of leaving a bigger mark on the cup than just the 'first female' footnote. I had ridden Brave Trespasser to a last-stride win at Moonee Valley two starts before over 2054 metres. That was usually the distance it took this tough stayer to get warm, so I knew he was at the top of his game. With his light weight and grinding stamina, Dad and I thought he could go close if the breaks went our way.

They didn't. When we got up on cup morning the temperamental Melbourne weather turned on the tears. By the time I got to Caulfield, two hours before the cup, the surface was so sodden Dad and I knew we had lost any chance of winning. Brave Trespasser couldn't handle slippery footing.

That eased the pressure as I sat in the female jockey's room, all alone, waiting for a childhood dream to come true. All I could do was give my horse the best possible chance and hope for a miracle.

When the barriers sprang open, I didn't worry about the frantic tussle up the straight that can make or break a winning Caulfield Cup ride. I just guided Brave Trespasser over to the rails at the tail of the field, letting him conserve his effort for the business end of the race.

Up ahead, Brent Thomson was giving a master class in how top jockeys make their reputations. From the outside barrier, he pushed forward steadily, tucking in behind the charge for the lead. Into the first turn, as everyone else slotted into position to avoid having to cover extra ground around the bend, Thomson pushed on to the front. He knew Lord Reims loved the mud, conditions that made it hard for the backmarkers to gain ground on the leaders quickly. Six hundred metres from home Thomson kicked clear, putting everything on the line. The cautious and those stuck in traffic would have their excuses, but all the glory was with Thomson and Lord Reims.

Brave Trespasser tried his best in the greasy ground, passing half a dozen runners in the straight to finish tenth.

For me, to have walked out into the same mounting yard as Harry White, Peter Cook, Pat Hyland and Brent Thomson was thrill enough. It was certainly a long way from pulling on my riding boots in a dingy broom closet at Mowbray on Caulfield Cup day seven years earlier.

Sixteen years on from Lord Reims' day of glory, as this book goes to print, that dog-eared 1987 Caulfield Cup race book has become a collector's item. Brave Trespasser, the 66 to 1 pop, is still the only horse in the race's 124-year history to be entrusted to a female jockey.

In some ways the lack of media fuss over my precedent-setting ride in the Caulfield Cup might have seemed like a sign of progress. The following month, when New Zealander Maree Lyndon became the first woman to ride in a Melbourne Cup, it looked as if racing was catching up with the outside world. Less than a decade after the first female apprentices signed up to be jockeys, women riders were mounting up in the two biggest events on the racing calendar. Yet since 1987, only one other female rider has been given the opportunity to ride in either of the big races—New Zealander Linda Ballantyne in the 1989 Melbourne Cup.

Plenty of talented Australian girls have staked a claim as apprentices but have not been given the opportunities on good horses after losing their apprentice's weight claim. The Payne sisters, Therese and Maree, are good examples. They were probably just as talented as their brother Paddy as apprentices. Paddy is now rated in the top handful of jockeys in the land and has ridden champions such as Tie the Knot and Northerly. I'm not knocking Paddy—I love the way he rides, letting his horses relax, waiting patiently until the right moment to make his move and coaxing, not thrashing, the best out of his mounts. We'll never know whether Therese or Maree could have done just as well. They didn't get the chance to learn how to control races on superior horses, and benefit from the confidence and credibility that comes with making big wins look easy.

It always seems to come back to the old bar room assumption that women aren't strong enough to make it as a jockey. What a joke! If you went into the male jockeys' room after a Melbourne Cup you would find at least half a dozen collapsed bags of skin and bone, utterly spent from having starved themselves to get their weight down. A fifteen-year-old girl could beat them in an arm wrestle in that state, let alone a fit, natural lightweight woman jockey. But until a female rider has a father with a horse good enough to win the big race, it seems the old boys' network will prevail.

Taking the plunge

10

Dad had his own dream. He had become a trainer almost by accident, but had found he loved the challenge and the competition of racing as much as the lifestyle. Like me, he felt he had proved himself at the top level in Tasmania and he wanted to test himself against the likes of Hayes and Cummings on the mainland.

The Victorian campaign in the spring of 1987 was not just about chasing the big cups with Brave Trespasser; Dad took four horses over to see how our team measured up to the mainland's best.

We based ourselves at Ballarat, a regional town an hour west of Melbourne. The country feel suited Dad, the horses and me much better than Flemington, where the turf royalty held court.

We were encouraged when our horse Kometa ran second at Bendigo and Brave Trespasser broke through for our first

Melbourne win at Moonee Valley. Brave Trespasser had done himself proud in the Caulfield Cup. Had he had his favoured firm ground, he would have finished a lot closer. Other horses of ours started off well but had bad luck: Remainder Man won a trial but then got injured and couldn't race. Trey Valve also hurt himself and managed only a couple of unplaced runs.

Despite these modest results, at least one Ballarat Turf Club committee man was impressed enough with our efforts to make it known that a property the club owned next to the course was available if we were interested.

Dad and I discussed it. We both thought we should go for it. The problem was we knew Mum wouldn't want to leave Tassie. She loved everything about the place. Ballarat was not a big city like Perth or even Hobart, but it still wasn't her cup of tea. Without telling her, Dad wrote a letter to the club expressing an interest in their block of land and asking for the financial details.

When we returned to Wesley Vale from the Melbourne campaign, we kept the Ballarat idea to ourselves. In January Dad rang the Ballarat committee man to see where we stood and was told that a couple of the Ballarat officials were coming over for Hobart Cup day. We didn't have a runner in the 1988 cup, but that day sealed our move to Ballarat. All three runners Dad lined up on the supporting card won. The committee men wouldn't take no for an answer. Dad could buy the block next to the track to build a house on, and the club would build stalls on an adjoining block, which we could lease.

When we finally worked up the courage to put it to Mum she was not impressed. The mainlanders would never accept me as a jockey on my merits, she said. Owners would not give their horses to a trainer whose stable jockey was a woman. It just wasn't worth the risk. We would have to drag her kicking and screaming out of Wesley Vale.

It was one of the toughest times we had had as a family. For Dad and I, it meant everything to make this move. But not without Mum.

She hated the idea of leaving Wesley Vale. Going to Victoria was the worst thing we could do, she thought, but she wasn't going to hold back her husband and only child if that was what they had their minds set on. Eventually she agreed to go, but she didn't pretend to like it.

I was so excited. After ten years of honing my craft I was off to play in the big league.

My boyfriend Brendon was also keen to go. He had made a name for himself by winning the prestigious Hiskens Steeplechase in Melbourne on the Tasmanian horse Tengah Hari, and moving to Victoria gave him the chance of staking a claim for other top jumpers.

Brendon and I had become engaged the previous year, on the night of my 21st birthday. That had allowed Brendon to move from the track rider's quarters where he'd been living up to the main house with me. We made our engagement public at a big party at the Devonport Surf Club for my 21st, which also happened to be the night I came out of my apprenticeship.

I wasn't in any hurry to get married. The engagement was just something we felt we should do after two and a half years of going steady, rather than a curtain-raiser to a wedding.

I told Brendon I wasn't going to be ready to hang up my riding boots and have babies for quite a while and he was fine with that. We were both more focused on the lure of making our names on the famous Melbourne racetracks than settling down to domestic bliss.

By the time Mum, Dad, Brendon and I moved into our new two-storey, four-bedroom brick home in Kennedy's Road in March 1989 things had become grim in Victoria—this was the beginning of Prime Minister Paul Keating's 'recession we had to have'. The interest rate on the sizeable loan Mum and Dad had to take out to set up the new operation was heading towards 16 per cent.

In our own minds we had come to Victoria as established players at the top of our profession, but it was as if we were starting out all over again. I thought I was entitled to bid for rides from the best stables—that seemed to be taken as a newcomer being a bit presumptuous. When I rang around trainers looking for rides there were few takers. At the big stables I didn't get past the foreman.

In a way I could understand it. It was only natural these stables would stick with the top riders who had been doing the job for them for years. And when the big stables sent horses up to the country, there were plenty of highly talented apprentices they could use who had the advantage of an apprentice's weight claim. The Freedman stable, for instance, which was then sweeping all before it, had just brought over a shy, teenaged apprentice named Damien Oliver from Perth. Within a couple of years he was vying for the premiership. (I got to know Damien on the country circuit and he was a friendly, down-to-earth young man who didn't lose those qualities once he'd tasted success.)

With the big stables out of reach, it was going to be up to Dad to provide me with the winners I would need to make my mark. He too found it harder to adjust to the new level of competition than he had expected. As a bricklayer, a soccer player, and a self-taught trainer, he had mastered new skills quickly. He had never failed at anything. He believed that with hard work and a little time to gather local experience, taking on the Victorian racing industry would be no different to any other task he'd set himself.

Dad had underestimated how little respect mainlanders give Tasmanians. Victorian owners didn't think success on the Apple Island counted for anything. They would rather give their horses to a Victorian with no notable victories than give them to Dad, who had a proven record of winning big races.

The other thing that took time to adjust to was the amount of racing and the sheer scale of the opposition on the mainland. In Tasmania there were a couple of hundred horses in training, most of which we knew by reputation, if not in the flesh. Here there were thousands. In Tasmania there was generally only one meeting a week. Here there were so many we had no idea which meetings would be strong and which would be weak.

Luck plays a big part in racing. We were having none. A couple of the most promising horses we brought over from Tasmania developed back problems. At home it hardly mattered if Dad lost a good horse to the injury list for a while—owners were always offering him another one to train, or the stock he had bought at the sales the year before would come through and make the grade. That wasn't happening at Ballarat.

It took four months to get our first winner. By then we really needed it. The bitterly cold Ballarat winter and the intrusion of other trainers' horses streaming past our front door was getting to Mum.

The lack of opportunity to break into the big time was getting to me. In my first six months in Victoria I had just nine winners.

The facilities for women jockeys at some tracks were abysmal. At the Hamilton course in the Western District the girls had to walk through the male jockeys' changing area to get to the weighing room. Somehow there was always at least one of them only half-dressed when one of the girls came through to use the scales.

I had been around long enough not to be intimidated. I'd look the near-naked ones right in the eye and say, 'G'day, how's your wife?', weigh myself and walk out in my own good time.

Therese Payne and her younger sister, Maree, were not so confident. Maree would only go in to use the scales if Therese went with her and vice versa. Their eyes tracked a fixed path across the floor until they got to the scales, flicked up quickly to see the reading, then went back to the floor until they made it back to the door. I suppose these days it would be called sexual harassment, but it was all in a spirit of fun.

At Horsham, the lady jockeys' room backed on to the stewards' office. One day I used this architectural quirk to my advantage. I had been involved in a mid-race skirmish and the stewards called me in to ask for my version of the incident. After I'd made the usual excuses, they asked me to wait outside while they deliberated. I raced back to the jockeys' room and put my ear to the wall. I heard one of them say they should charge me with careless riding 'and see what happens'.

When the stewards called me back in, I didn't wait for them to read out the charge. In my sternest tone I said: 'If you charge me I will appeal and I will get off because there is simply no justification and you know it.' No charge was laid.

It was hard going for that first year, but in the winter of 1990 I got a lucky break. Bert Newton, the TV host and keen racing man, invited me on to his show. During the interview Bert dropped the fact that he owned horses and had used a woman trainer, Kath Johnson. Quick as a flash, I put him on the spot in front of his adoring audience—he could hardly refuse an invitation to use a female jockey as well.

It worked. Bert put me on his horse Predominate at Bendigo. We finished down the track. Bert kept faith in me though, and gave me the ride for Predominate's next start, at Flemington. This time we romped home at 40 to 1. It was only a midweek meeting in July, but still a big notch in my belt to win at 'headquarters' for the first time.

Finally, the phone started to ring with offers of good rides. The only trouble was, now I had to turn them down. I had already accepted a trip to Japan for a series of lady riders' races in August and the chance to pick up good prizemoney, all expenses paid.

I loved every minute of my month in Japan. Everything from the sumo to the sushi—well, not so much the sushi.

For a start, the weather was hot, thawing me out from frostbitten Ballarat. I rode morning trackwork in a T-shirt.

Tokyo was so different to any city I had seen. The skyscrapers went on forever. The streets were always teeming with people, even late at night when I sneaked out after our supposed curfew.

There were four Japanese in the series, along with two New Zealand girls, Linda Ballantyne and Kim Clapperton, myself and another Australian, Lyn Honan.

I found the Japanese girls, despite the language barrier, both fascinating and fun to be with. Their outlook on life could not have been more different from mine. They accepted without question that, being female, they were inferior to men. For one of the Japanese girls, this series was going to be her last outing on the track. She was about to marry a Japanese jockey. She would have to retire to look after his needs, she said. I just could not comprehend that. When I got married I was going to be an equal partner with the right to make my own choices about my career.

The racing was also a whole new experience. For a start, the tracks were made of packed dirt, as in the United States, not grass. With the dirt being continuously kicked up at the runners back in the field, the horses raced much further apart than in Australia. The crowds were so large and noisy the horses wore ear muffs.

The only problem I had was with the language. All the foreign girls had interpreters to translate the trainer's riding instructions. For one of my rides, the interpreter said the horse needed to be hit with the whip to do his best. At least that's what I understood him to say. Apparently the message was supposed to be that the horse was very sensitive to the whip, so go easy on it.

Coming into the straight we were right up with the leaders. I pulled the whip and let go of a couple of heavy cracks. My mount was whip-sensitive all right. So sensitive he almost galloped out of his skin, bolting away to win by six lengths.

After another race I was called in to see the stewards about some interference. The stewards couldn't speak English. I didn't speak a word of Japanese. There was no interpreter. They talked to me very sternly. I gave my version of what happened. Neither side registered a word of what the other had said. I still don't know whether I was reprimanded, suspended or cleared.

By the end of the month I was missing the family. I had enjoyed the experience of such a different culture and, more importantly, I had picked up about $10 000 from the series. We were going to need it. By the time I got back to Ballarat no one remembered that easy win on Predominate at Flemington. I was back begging for rides.

More and more, our financial fortunes at Ballarat came to rest on my riding success. Even deciding which meetings to ride at became an accounting exercise: On Monday there might be a meeting 150 kilometres away where you had five or six OK rides. Tuesday's meeting might be a 250-kilometre drive away, with only two rides booked, but both looking like reasonable chances. If you get beaten in both rides though, the riding fees won't cover the cost of the petrol. Solution: You ride on Monday, stay home on Tuesday.

My method of dealing with the financial pressures and the frustration of not making the impact I had hoped in Victoria was to block out the grim reality and try even harder. I bottled up my disappointment and put all my energy into every ride.

Brendon had had some early success, but at the end of the first year in Victoria he broke his leg badly in two places in a fall at Warrnambool, putting him out of action for a few months. With him at home recovering, and me on the road most of the week chasing rides, we began to drift apart. I found out Brendon was seeing a female strapper on the side. In response to this I started going out after the races with some of the guys, and a couple of times I went home with one on a one-night stand.

I still wanted things to work out with Brendon though. I decided to confront the strapper. I went to her flat and warned her that if she didn't back off she would be sorry.

Brendon had a hurdle rider mate he hung out with and one night they decided to go out camping. I drove them to their camp site and helped them set up their tents, but something about the way they were acting made me suspicious.

I drove home and went to bed, getting up at 5.30 a.m. to start work mucking out the horse boxes and riding track-work. When I finished, around 9 a.m., I decided to pay a visit to the happy campers. As I pulled into the camp site I saw a familiar silver car—the strapper's.

Brendon must have heard me arrive because he scrambled out of his tent in his underwear.

'Hi,' he said, planting himself between me and his tent. 'Do you mind going down to the shop to get us some breakfast?'

'Sure,' I said. 'Do you want to come with me?'

As soon as he turned to go back into the tent to get his clothes, I dived past him and ripped open the tent flap. Sure enough, there was the strapper tucked up under the blankets. I threw myself on top of her and tore at her hair. Brendon grabbed me by the legs and hauled me out of the tent. While I wrestled with him the strapper escaped to her car.

She had a good head start by the time I threw Brendon off, but I had a V-8 Commodore against her four-cylinder sedan so I soon rounded her up, slamming my brakes on in front of her car to make her pull up.

She desperately pushed down the locks of her doors but I was scrambling across her back seat before she could cover all four of them. I flew at her in a blind rage. I think that all the things I'd suppressed—the stalling of my career, the money worries, the unravelling of my relationship with Brendon— just boiled over at that moment and I lashed out with punch after punch.

That night the police knocked on my door. The strapper had been taken to hospital with a broken cheekbone. The officers took me to the station and told me it would be better for me if I told them everything. I did and was duly charged with assault. The magistrate put me on twelve months' probation.

By then I had told Brendon to pack his bags. He went home to Tassie, but after a couple of months we talked out our problems on the phone and agreed to give it another chance. He moved back in with me at Ballarat, but things were never quite the same.

The ironic outcome of all this was that breaking the strapper's cheekbone actually boosted my standing with the local trainers. In their eyes, I'd shown I was tough enough to do the business for them and I began getting more outside rides.

The Buckinghams weren't the only ones doing it hard at the turn of the decade. The Pyramid Building Society collapse at the beginning of 1990 had devastated the communities in and around Geelong. Soaring interest rates were running small towns into the ground right across the State.

When I turned up to ride at any country race meeting now, I was lining up against desperate men. They didn't have a lot of style in the saddle, these blokes, but they had children to feed and clothe, mortgages in arrears and more than likely a brother, sister, mother or father in the same boat. They taught me an important skill—how to ride with desperation.

On this circuit, where you ate according to your day's results, you played for keeps. If you were on a strong winning chance, and had drawn a barrier that should give you the perfect position behind the leader, you didn't just bounce your horse out and wait for everyone to fall into place around you. You *forced* your way into that prime position. And when you needed a gap coming to the home turn, you didn't wait for one to appear, you *pushed* your way through.

When I started riding I shunned using the whip, believing I could get the best out of a horse by being kind to it. Part of the art of desperation riding is knowing that some horses need a crack or two with the stick to pull out their best. I carried two whips with me, one that was only used for flicking at horses I knew would try their hearts out, and one for those that needed a good whack. When a horse had more to give in a tight finish, I could get it.

The prizemoney at these country meetings was not enough to provide everyone with a living. Betting 'plunges' would make or break the balance sheet for many stables. We had never been big punters on our own horses. Dad might have $200 each way if he thought he had one that was ready to win at generous odds, but we never had a spare few thousand we could afford to lose if we went for a 'plunge' and it didn't come off.

I didn't put myself under any great pressure when there was a 'big go' on a horse I was riding. If the owners and trainer wanted to take that risk, that was their choice.

I did feel sorry for one owner-trainer, Beverley Vermay, who put me on Spirit Raiser, a 25 to 1 shot at Wangaratta one day. The connections had put enough on the horse to pay off the mortgage. Spirit Raiser was ready for the job. I settled him midfield, and in the straight he stormed home to pass every horse bar one. His backers had to be content with a small profit they made from the place dividend, but they should have got the house—two weeks later the winner was disqualified for returning a positive drug swab.

It has always angered me that a few rotten eggs in the racing game can taint everyone involved. Since I started riding, there has been a corrupt element trying to fix races by buying off jockeys or doping horses. The stewards scrutinise jockeys so closely now it's hard to get away with anything blatant, but the fact is that in any business with big money at stake you're going to get people greedy and stupid enough to try to rip the system off. And some still get away with it. No matter how much drug testing the stewards do, the crooks are always one step ahead with a new substance that can't be detected or that can be masked by something else.

When I started riding, one of the reasons I was so unpopular with some of the veteran jockeys was that I unwittingly thwarted some of their scams. When a stable set a horse for a betting coup, the jockey would let his mates know so they could give the 'money' horse a clear passage. I wasn't let in on the secret, and when I swooped home to beat a 'plunge' horse I'd get the filthiest looks from the old boys' network as we trotted back after the race.

I was never actually asked to make sure my mount got beaten, but there was one time in my early years I was asked to pull a trick that made me furious. A successful trainer legged me up on his horse and said: 'This will win. When you go for him in the straight, use the butt of your whip on his neck.'

I knew exactly what was going on. In training, the horse would have been given an electric shock on its neck at the end of its gallops with a battery-powered device called a 'jigger', sending it into a galloping frenzy. By stabbing it on the neck on race day, my job was to spook the horse into thinking it had been zapped so it would charge through the pain barrier.

I knew this horse would be fit and ready to win if the stable was counting on him to clean out the bookies, so I rode him confidently in front. Down the straight, the favourite cruised up alongside us. I had promised myself I'd do everything I could to protect my horse from the trauma of the 'jigger'. I gave him a couple of cuts with the whip on the backside, which was enough to push us ahead of the challenger. The favourite's jockey went for his whip and he nosed ahead of us. I'd sworn not to dig the whip-butt into my poor horse's neck, but my competitive instincts wouldn't let me give the race up so I compromised and slapped his neck with the side of the whip. Whoosh! He surged to the post to win comfortably.

The trainer and his mates got their money, but they could tell I didn't want to be part of this sort of sting. Word soon got around that I couldn't be trusted to play ball.

Being on the outer when it came to that sort of thing probably left me a little bit naïve as to some of what went on when I was riding. I remember in my second year at Ballarat being invited back to Tassie to ride in a special jockeys' challenge race featuring some of the top riders from around the country. We were all put up at the Wrest Point casino and after dinner, the night before the race, a mainland jockey invited a friend and me into the high rollers' room. Our jaws dropped as we watched the jockey who had invited us to lose hand after hand at $500 a throw. He didn't seem too worried—he upped the bet to $1000 a hand. Within minutes he was down $10 000. This was way out of my league and I quickly made my excuses and left.

I had seen before what gambling losses could do to people with a weakness. A jockey I knew got on a losing streak, wasted all his own money, then stole from his partner. His partner forgave him once, but the second time she caught him it ended their relationship. Before that I'd been happy to put $10 in a poker machine and play until I lost it—it was just a bit of fun. After what happened to my friend, I looked at the pokie players glued to their machines as if in a trance in a new light. I could see how quickly they could become addicted, chasing the rush of that next win, and I knew the pain they were going to cause themselves and their loved ones. I won't go near a poker machine now.

By the end of the 1990–91 season I had found form and was doing nicely on the country and provincial circuits. I rode a few doubles that season and scored my first treble, at St Arnaud, where I went within a short head of making it four for the day.

But at the end of the season, after two years at Ballarat, we reluctantly raised the white flag. Dad still believed he had the ability to match the Victorian trainers, but without the quality of horses they had, it was a matter of making a strategic withdrawal or losing everything we had built up.

It was a sad day when the 'For Sale' sign went up at Kennedy's Road, especially for Dad. For the first time in his life he felt like a loser—although not a quitter. He vowed we would be back one day with the horseflesh to prove Tasmanians had what it took.

I could have stayed and made a go of it, but the Buckinghams had always been a team. We took a chance together, now we'd pay the price together.

Record books and wedding bells

11

Although our Victorian adventure had not turned out the way we hoped, there was no doubt it had made me a much more accomplished rider.

My new skills took a while to show up on the scoreboard, though. Most of the horses Dad shipped back to Tassie caught a virus on the boat. That meant he had few runners in the early months of our first season back, 1991–92.

While I had been away, the ex-Victorian Stephen Maskiell had become almost as dominant as Max Baker in his heyday. I finished second to him that first year back and had to live in his shadow the following year as he set a new state record for winners in a season—93.

In 1993–94 we had a neck-and-neck battle. Coming into the last month, Stephen led by ten wins, but then he got suspended. I had four meetings to catch up with him. I rode three winners at the first meeting, two at the second, three at the third. In that sort of form, coming into the last meeting I still had a chance of getting the two wins I needed for the title. I came up empty-handed, so I was runner-up again.

I had had enough of running second—it was now more than a decade since I had won my lone premiership. I made a decision that things would change, and from then on, they did. I started the 1994–95 season firing, and the guns didn't stop blazing until I broke the 100-winner barrier, the first time it had been done in Tasmania. My winning total of 109 winners still stands as the State's riding record for a season.

Just about everything went right for me that year. I stabilised my diet to ride at 52 kilos, so I didn't have to suffer the mental and physical trauma of losing 10 per cent of my bodyweight each week.

I had a new man in my life, too. I had finally broken up with Brendon on my 28th birthday, in March 1993, seven years after our engagement. (I should see if I can get that added to my list of records—longest engagement not to end in marriage.)

We had split up and got back together a few times since we came back from Ballarat. When we were first engaged I thought that by the time I was 30 I would have found fortune and fame as a jockey and would be ready to give up riding, settle down, get married and take over the training duties from Dad. At 28, I could see that wasn't going to happen. And even when that time did come, I could see it wasn't going to be with Brendon, so I broke it off with him. I still care for him, and we keep in touch—after my fall, he was one of the few people I let in to see me. But by 1993, we had well and truly run our race.

The way I met the man who would become my husband reads a bit like how Mum and Dad got together. In early 1994, Mum and I went to visit some horses at Helen Richardson's property. We trained for Helen, former wife of Greg Richardson, who was Brave Trespasser's owner, and when her horses were having a break from training they went back to her place.

Helen's nephew Jason King was there the day we visited, but I didn't fancy him at first glance—it was his friend who caught my eye. Mum and I had a girly chat about these two new young men on the way home. Jason, dark-haired and full of life at 21, was a bit of all right, Mum said.

A few weeks later there was a karaoke party after the Spreyton races. I knew Brendon would be there with his new girlfriend and I didn't want to turn up on my own. Mum suggested asking Jason—'No shame in turning up with a younger man on your arm.'

Jason was a charmer, confident for his age and an enthusiastic party-goer. We had a ball at the karaoke night, with none of the clammy nervousness that can make a first date excruciating.

On Monday he sent me a dozen red roses, a romantic move not included in the courtship manual used by most Tasmanian men. I was impressed. We saw each other every night that week.

The first night I arrived to pick him up, he said he was afraid to come out of the house because he'd never had such a beautiful woman waiting out in the driveway. We talked and talked all that night about everything from our favourite music to the Big Bang theory of the creation of the universe. I had always been fascinated by outer space—I'm convinced there must be life out there—and gazing up at the stars, I poured my heart out to Jason about the universe and the endless possibilities within it.

By the end of the week we were hopelessly in love. Two months later we were engaged.

When your life is all roses off the track, things tend to go your way on it as well (and vice versa). And lady luck was looking out for me.

In the 1996 Hobart Cup, I was booked to ride Vaudeville Piper, a 14 to 1 chance. The Saturday before the cup he had his last lead-up run in Hobart. That night, my jockey friend Dianne Parish drove me home from the races. Kim had retired from riding by then, so Di, who was based in Georgetown, became my travelling partner to the races.

She was quite different to Kim, petite and always smiling. Her husband has multiple sclerosis, but she never brooded on it, and was always the one cracking jokes. Like me, she liked fast cars and we took it in turns to drive each other to the races in our Celicas. She didn't have children either, so whenever one of us had a big win we went out on the town together.

On the way home from Hobart we were following the truck carrying Vaudeville Piper and five other horses. Around 8 p.m. we were right behind the truck on the Midlands Highway, when, just as Di was about to pull out and overtake the truck, it suddenly drifted across to the middle of the road. It kept going, across three lanes, until it was travelling on the far shoulder of the oncoming lane.

The metal canopy of the tray carrying the horses managed to hit the one big branch overhanging the road, knocking the tray over as the cab ploughed on ahead for a few hundred metres into a paddock.

Di screeched to a halt and we ran across to the crash scene. It was bedlam. The float was on its side and the horses trapped inside were in terror. Some were already dead when we got there. I cradled one in my arms, trying to soothe it by whispering in its ear. I don't know how long I sat there stroking its head and neck before the quickened breaths slowed to a weak pant, then stopped altogether.

That left only one of the six horses alive, Vaudeville Piper. He was bleeding from the nostrils, still trapped in the wreckage. 'Come on Vaudey,' I said, resting his head in my lap. 'You can't die on me now.'

For what seemed like a couple of hours I kept talking to him as rescuers with bolt cutters hacked away the twisted metal entombing him. Even when he was freed he was unable to get to his feet. 'If he doesn't get up in a few minutes, we'll have to put him down,' someone said. That was all the motivation he needed. At about 10 p.m. we scrambled him up the embankment to be taken to the Hagley Equine Hospital.

I went to see him the next day. 'Vaudey' was totally blind from a blow to the head, but in time he recovered his sight and was able to race again. There would be no Hobart Cup for him that year, though. Or for me, it seemed.

A couple of days later the secretary of the Tasmanian Racing Club, Colin Bellchambers, rang to say he had heard that one of that year's Victorian raiders, Ken Keys, was looking for a rider for his horse Jam City. I rang the Cranbourne trainer and he agreed to give me the ride.

He sent over videotapes of Jam City's recent races, which showed a headstrong horse. In most of his races Jam City pulled his way to the lead, leaving himself short of energy for a sprint at the finish. I was always confident I could get this sort of horse to settle, so I thought he would have a good chance in the cup.

Mum and I decided to create some good karma by invoking Vaudeville Piper, the lucky sole survivor of the float crash. We went to work on the bloodied white shirt I was wearing when I helped to haul him out of the wreckage. Mum had to bleach and dye it to get the colour back—even the gold trim had turned pink from the blood.

Wearing the shirt to cup day gave me a good feeling. And as soon as I climbed aboard Jam City, I knew my luck was in. He was feeling so well he gave a squeal as we cantered down to the starting barriers, then let rip with a double-barrelled 'pig root' kick with his back legs.

Jam City jumped out well, keen to be up with the pace. I had him settled nicely, but when the pace slowed he started to pull, so I let him go up onto the heels of the runner in front, which almost tripped him over. That gave him the necessary shock to back off and race kindly. From then on we enjoyed the run of the race behind the leader on the rails. This time Jam City had plenty in reserve to hold off the challengers at the finish.

Six days before, I had been traumatised watching a bloodied horse die in my arms. My supposed Hobart Cup mount,

Vaudeville Piper, was lucky to be alive, let alone run. Now here I was on top of the world, with my name back on the State's most prized racing trophy after an absence of ten years.

Di and I shared a drink out of the cup as we drove home that night.

By the end of the season, I hadn't come anywhere near my century of the previous year, but my 64 winners were enough to take out my third Tasmanian premiership.

On 13 April 1997, Jason and I got married after three years of living together.

The eight-year age difference didn't bother either of us. After the worldly worries of the Ballarat years, it was refreshing for me to be with someone who was not tied down by responsibilities, who took life one day at a time. For him, it was an exciting step into the life of one of the state's highest profile sporting stars; cheering home his new girlfriend to a win at the races, then celebrating long into the night.

Jason had been working at the Wesley Vale pulp and paperboard mill as a general hand when we started going out. The money wasn't great and he lived at home with his parents. He only seemed to have one pair of shoes, a dusty pair of runners.

Mum and I decided that if he was going to be my new escort around town we would have to upgrade his wardrobe. For his birthday we fitted him out with stylish leather boots, some smart new clothes and a gold chain around his neck. Before he came on holiday with us to the Gold Coast, Jason had not been out of Tasmania.

The most important thing I bought him was an intercom system for his parents' house. Jason was a chronic asthmatic. The dusty environment of the board mill constantly irritated his condition. A couple of times he had attacks in the night and had to crawl down the hall to knock on his parents' door before being rushed to hospital.

Jason appreciated all the treats I was able to give him, but his mother did not seem so pleased to have an older, independent woman taking him out on the town until 2 a.m. Jason's parents were outwardly nice to me, but there was a distance between us right from the start.

That distance—physically and emotionally—opened further when we told them about our engagement, and further still the following month when Jason moved in with me at our property at Latrobe which, in the spirit of returning to our racing roots in Tassie, we had named Brigadoon.

Although Jason's Aunty Helen was keen on horses, he was frightened of them. When you live with the Buckinghams, though, you can hardly avoid horses, and as Jason spent more time around the stables he got used to them. He liked to go hunting with his mates, but when he saw how much I loved animals and heard my views on shooting trips he gave them up.

Because of his asthma, and the frequent night shifts at the board mill, I wanted him to give up working there. The solution was obvious—he could help out in the stables at our place.

Mum and Dad were happy to have Jason on board. Jason became a solid stable hand, although he lacked the touch of a natural horse lover.

After living together for three years, we were both confident of being soulmates for life and felt ready to tie the knot. The wedding was a small affair, just his parents, my parents and a celebrant. I didn't want a media circus to spoil such a personal day.

I wore a smart, pale cream suit that Mum gave me. After the ceremony we invited a dozen of our closest friends to our house, including Kim Simpson, who by now had married Lenny Dixon, Greg and Helen Richardson, and Jason's sister and her husband. It was lovely to be able to share the day with the important people in our lives.

The next day, before the news hit the media, I sought out Brendon at Spreyton, where he was riding trackwork after retiring as a jockey. I didn't want him to find out I was married from reading the papers. He said he was happy for me and wished me all the best—which meant a lot to me.

Jason and I took a ten-day Pacific cruise on the *Fair Princess* for our honeymoon. In Noumea, I shopped for French lingerie. In Vanuatu, Jason and I took a guided trek along a riverside track to a beautiful waterfall. It was every girl's dream, the perfect start to the rest of our life together.

After the cruise, it was back to business through the long, cold Tassie winter, waiting for the high stakes excitement of the big summer races.

Winning my third Hobart Cup, on L'Espion in February 1998, was the highlight of that carnival. At the beginning of May, Jason and I set off with Kim and Lenny for our annual getaway to Queensland. When we got back, Mum and Dad took their turn to escape.

I liked the stints as acting trainer when Dad was away. I felt by now I had mastered riding. Steering a fit, focused, content racehorse around a racetrack takes a couple of minutes. Getting it fit, focused and content takes months, even years. It was always my goal to be a trainer after my riding career ended, but at 33, with our financial setbacks from Ballarat having put us behind, I was still five or six years away from being able to hang up my saddle.

When Dad got home, I was able to report I had won for him on Kimbia's Gold, my 906th winner as a jockey.

I said to Dad: 'What's to stop me riding 1000?'

'Nothing,' he said.

And that's the way I felt when I looked at my book of rides for that ill-fated meeting at Elwick on 30 May 1998. My first ride would be for Royston Carr, a good friend for many years. He had a chestnut mare entered for the first race. Royston thought she had some ability even though she had never won. With my confidence so high—I was riding a winner every four rides or so—I thought I could get her up to win even though I had never been on her before. I would have remembered such a pretty name: Theutelle.

Brave new world. Mum and I enjoy the sunny West Australian climate after our move from England.

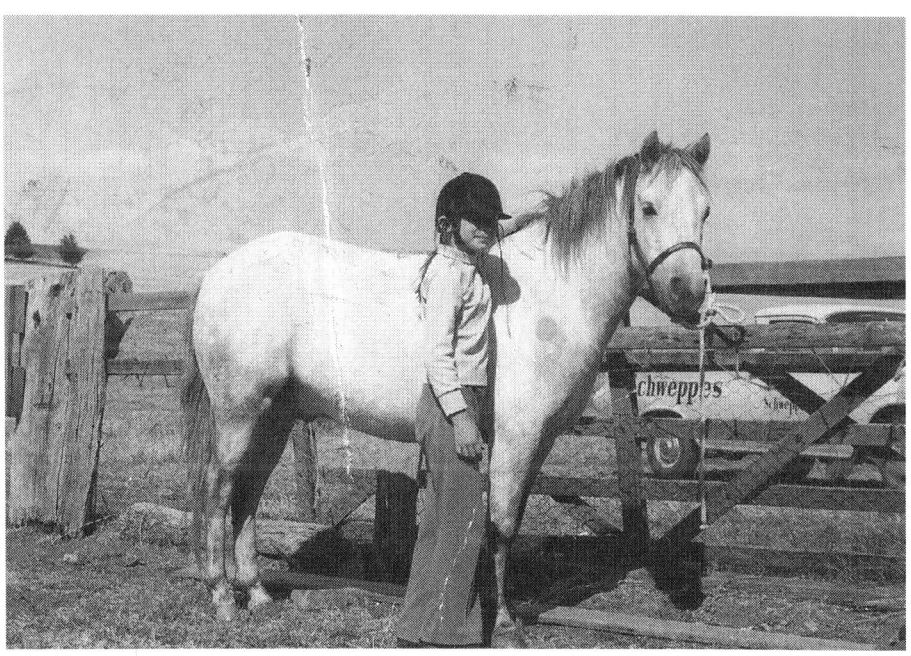

Mounting up. My first pony, Mavournie.

Above: **Horse sense.** I was warned to stay clear of the retired Caulfield Cup winner, Beer Street, but I soon had him eating out of my hand.
(Courtesy *The Advocate*)

Opposite: **Trailblazer.** Dad's first racehorse, Brigadoon Boy, was the matchmaker of our family to the racing industry. (Photo *The Examiner Press*)

My 'Boy'. Winning on Brigadoon Boy, the horse I learned to ride on, was one of my biggest thrills.

Above: **Queen of the Turf.** As an apprentice I was invited to ride in a special race against top jockeys, including Gary Willetts (far left) and Roy Higgins (far right).

Opposite: **Making history.** The presentation of my first Tasmanian Jockeys' premiership, at the age of 17. (Courtesy *The Mercury*)

Above: **Bolting in.** Winning my first Hobart Cup, in 1986, on Dark Intruder, trained by Dad. (Courtesy *The Mercury*)

Left: **Winners are grinners.** Dad and I celebrate after Dark Intruder's victory. (Courtesy *The Mercury*)

Far left: **A classy stallion.** 'Gary' taught me so much about how to ride a good horse. (Courtesy Herald and Weekly Times Photographic Collection)

Overleaf: **Home, sweet home.** Back to Brigadoon, with Dad and Benson, after leaving hospital. (Photo Chris Crerar)

PART THREE

AFTER
THE FALL

My left foot

You can't feel sorry for yourself for too long in a ward full of paraplegics and quadriplegics. There's always someone worse off than you.

When I left intensive care I went to ward 13 EW, a clearing house for 'paras' and 'quads' before they left the Austin hospital.

On one side of me was John, a paraplegic who lost the use of his legs many years ago. He was back in hospital after a big night out at the pub. He had been having a great time, drinking and entertaining a girl sitting in his lap. In hindsight, he realised her weight on top of his own considerable bulk must have led to the wheels of his wheelchair buckling in. Because when John wheeled himself home from the pub every turn sliced into his thigh. John, like me when the horse galloped over my legs, did not feel a thing. Not the wheel churning through his flesh nor the blood running down his legs. He would be in 13 EW until the stitches to the deep lacerations in his thighs healed.

On the other side of me was a lady who was a complete quadriplegic below her third vertebrae. She had had a car accident twenty years before in which her fiancé was killed. The only parts of her body she could move were her head and her neck. She used these to the full, painting with a brush clenched between her teeth. We shared a few jokes at John's expense. He was a shocking snorer and we would stage-whisper about how we couldn't wait for him to get the OK to go home.

As they'd had so much more experience of disability, I was keen to ask both of them about their experiences. They answered very matter-of-factly and seemed to be not the least bit bitter about what had happened to them.

Then one night when I couldn't get to sleep, I called out to see if anyone else was awake. They both were. We were chatting away and out of nowhere I popped the big one: 'Don't you ever cry, don't you ever get upset and think about what you've lost?'

They both said, 'No'.

'Why not?' I said. 'It's terrible what has happened.'

The ward went quiet.

The next morning they both admitted they had had a quiet cry during the night. A wave of guilt ran through me. Here was I, the new kid on the block, stirring things up for two people who must have had to put their demons to rest many times already.

Day by day, I was edging out of the anger phase into acceptance. I was going out in my wheelchair most days for a short spell in the fresh air. The new facts of my life really hit home one day when a van pulled up with a motorised platform that could be lowered from an open sliding door to hoist a person in a wheelchair inside.

'Perhaps we could get one of those for me,' I said to Dad.

Most of the time, I shut out thoughts of the future. This was the way I'd coped during other traumatic times, such as when we had money worries at Ballarat. I had known then that dwelling on the problem would only put me under stress when I needed to be concentrating 100 per cent on winning.

In 13 EW I focused on the baby steps of progress I was making. For instance, when I arrived on the ward I couldn't change the channel on my TV because I had no power in my fingers to push the control buttons. The occupational therapist added a finger support to my right hand splint, which held my forefinger out straight. Using the power of my shoulder muscles, I could push the channel change button. It was a small thing, but even that did wonders for my sense of independence when I could do so little else.

Another small boost came from a trick I taught myself. Now that I was able to eat solid food and was being encouraged to put on weight for the first time in my life, I went on a lolly binge. I asked all my visitors to bring me sweets, especially round ones. I could wedge the packet in my left hand, tip a lolly—Maltesers were my favourite—onto the back of my right hand and use the forefinger of my left to roll the treat up the outside of my right arm to my shoulder. Then, with a shrug of the shoulder, the little chocolate-covered ball was close enough to suck into my mouth.

With the breathing tube gone, my taste buds recovered. I discovered I loved hospital food. I ate every scrap of every meal. Soon I was stacking on the weight.

The surroundings in 13 EW were much more pleasant than in the intensive care unit. I was able to get a bed near a window with a small balcony outside. The ward was strictly temperature controlled. The spinal cord regulates the body's response to temperature changes, and my cooling system was definitely impaired because I often felt unbearably hot. Mum, Dad, Kim or Jason could open the window to cool me down.

I had graduated from having a sponge bath in my bed to showering in a private cubicle. I would be wheeled in on a trolley and lowered into a shallow bath under the shower head. The unfamiliar sensation of water falling on my body gave me a wonderful cleansing feeling.

To empty my bowels, I had to be wheeled into the bathroom after being given a laxative, or a nurse had to pull on a glove and stimulate my back passage. Either way there was no privacy because I couldn't clean my own bottom.

One morning a nurse took me to the bathroom for my morning toilet stop. I couldn't go straight away so the nurse said she would come back in a few minutes. I don't know how long she was gone—it could have been five minutes or fifteen—because I fell into a panic attack. Sitting up on the commode, the supporting seat on top of the toilet, made me dizzy. The claustrophobia of being in the tiny room made it worse and I felt so nauseous I thought I was about to pass out. I lunged at the emergency button on the wall but it was a frustrating few centimetres out of reach. I felt so distressed my heart rate zoomed up and I could hardly breathe.

When the nurse came back, I refused to stay in the bath-room for my shower and they had to give me a sponge bath. For the next couple of days I would not get up on the commode again in case I fell into the grip of another panic attack. The worst thing about it was discovering what it is like to live with constant fear. I had never been frightened of anything—physically or mentally—until now.

Mum and Kim were using a self-contained flat across the road from the hospital. Most days, whichever one of them was staying there would take me for a wheelchair ride around the grounds and sometimes I would have lunch in the flat.

It was nice to go there and have some privacy, but even in this little haven there was no escaping what had brought us here. One day Mum cooked me a lunch of steak and chips, something I should have relished after living on taste-less, textureless fluids for so long. But all I felt up to doing was lying down on the bed. When I did go to sit up, I pooed myself. Being incontinent always upset me and having escaped the hospital for a special treat with Mum only to have this happen was the last straw. I burst into tears. Mum laid me down and cleaned me up, just as she had when I was a baby.

'I'm so sorry,' I whimpered. 'I'm so sorry.'

Mum stroked my arm and calmed me until I fell asleep.

Despite these bad patches, my spirits were gradually rising overall. My sense of humour had returned. I got Kim to scribble an addition to the medication chart at the bottom of my bed: 'Vodka as required'.

The day I moved into 13 EW I had interviews with the three big TV networks to promote a fundraising appeal the Tasmanian racing industry had set up for me. Dad had let most of his horses go so he could spend time with me in hospital. Our income had gone to virtually nil and we were living off our savings.

When the appeal was first launched I was still in intensive care. Channel Nine's early morning show hosted by Richard Wilkins and Tracey Grimshaw did a live interview with Jason from my bedside. I had an earpiece that allowed me to hear Wilkins' questions from the studio in Sydney but because of the ventilator tube I couldn't say a word.

When Wilkins asked about the outlook for the future, Jason, no doubt trying to keep my spirits up, said I was such a fighter I would walk again without a doubt, and maybe I would even ride again. If you watch the tape you can see my eyes flicking from the camera to Jason and back. I was desperate to butt in and shut Jason up. Here we were kicking off a fundraising appeal for a jockey whose career appeared to be ruined forever and her husband is telling the audience she'll make a full recovery, no worries!

In my interviews after moving to 13 EW, I stressed that although I was determined to get my body into the best shape possible, my only hope of working with horses again was through training, not riding.

In a funny way I found dealing with the media crews easier than facing people I knew. Even after leaving intensive care, no one apart from family and my closest friends was allowed in to visit. I hated the idea of people seeing me so helpless.

It was made worse by some of the weirdos who tried to bluff their way in. One man rang saying he was my 'real' father and then tried to get in to the ward by saying he was my brother.

Eventually we decided to use the password 'Elvis'—unless you knew it, you didn't get past the front desk or the switchboard.

Unfortunately there were some people we did want to contact who we couldn't reach. Among the hundreds of cards and letters that came, there was a group of special ones Mum put to one side. One was from a man who had so many frequent flyer points he couldn't use them all, so he gave them to Mum, Dad and Jason so they could fly over and rotate the bedside watch every few days. Somehow this precious pile of letters went missing and I never got to thank those wonderful people.

Sleeping through the night was still difficult. I had developed a severe pressure sore on the back of my head from my head collar, and the beds in 13 EW seemed rock-hard. I had to be turned at regular intervals throughout the night.

The World Cup soccer tournament was under way in France and it was a godsend for an insomniac who loved sport. The theme song for the tournament was Ricky Martin's 'La Copa Del Vida'. I loved that song. There is something about the way those Latin boys sing that just makes you want to dance.

One night, as the local TV station was crossing to France and Ricky was belting out his anthem, I thought: 'I should try to move.'

Within a few seconds I swore a tiny muscle deep in my inner thigh started twitching to the beat. It only lasted a moment, but I was convinced it was a muscle and it was moving. I could hardly believe it—I knew the medicos wouldn't.

My physio Jacquie had told me that as the spinal swelling went down, some distorted messages would start getting through, causing muscles to go into spasm. This was not to be confused with normal transmission being restored.

When Jason came in the next day, I told him my exciting news but ordered him to keep it a secret. I knew the medicos would just say it was a spasm and I didn't want Mum and Dad getting any false hope. I concentrated really hard to try to stir the inner thigh muscle so Jason could feel it for himself.

'Put your hand on it,' I told Jason. 'Can you feel it, can you feel it move?'

'I think so,' he said. 'I'm not sure.'

I was. And I was sure it was not just wishful thinking.

Jason went home a couple of days later to allow Dad to take up the vigil in 13 EW. Jacquie had shown Dad how to give me a therapeutic massage. He started on the arms, working down into the finger muscles, between the finger joints, then onto my thighs and calves and into the ankles. One day he swore he felt one of my fingers move, but I hadn't sensed anything.

A day or two later, he was near the end of the workout, rubbing my toes, bending them back towards my ankle, when the big toe of my left foot twitched back at him. We both felt this one. Our eyes locked in a moment's stunned silence.

'Bev, your toe, it moved!' he said. 'See if you can do it again.'

I concentrated hard, and when the toe twitched, I pushed with it and controlled the movement. Dad let out a cheer as big as if he'd just trained the winner of the Melbourne Cup. I was giggling like a little girl.

Dad raced out onto the balcony to call Mum on his mobile phone. As he was talking, he'd lean around the doorway to check on me, reporting every wiggle.

'She's doing it now, Joan,' he said. 'You can see them move. She just did it again!'

We were so excited we told the medical staff, but they played it down. They discouraged me from trying to exaggerate spasms. They said the spasms could get out of hand to the point where I could throw myself out of bed.

I didn't listen to them. I knew I could control the spasms. I could feel them coming on and when my toe twitched I could accentuate the movement.

Dad went home a couple of days later and it was Mum's turn to see the first signs of recovery. By now I could wiggle a few toes.

'What about your hands, Bev?' Mum said. 'Try moving your fingers.'

I'd been so overjoyed at the toe breakthrough I hadn't thought of that.

I concentrated really hard and, lo and behold, my left thumb moved sideways. Just a millimetre or two, but it was definitely voluntary movement. No spasm about it.

'Wow!' I cried. 'Look at that.'

Mum's eyes nearly popped out of her head in disbelief.

The next week was very exciting as the little symphony of movements built up.

Mum, Dad and Kim had been giving me an exercise that involved raising my leg and flexing the knee. I now managed to generate a bit of pressure against their shoulders with my leg.

Still the doctors stuck their fingers in their ears, denying any prospect that this could be the beginning of a significant recovery. Jacquie was the only one willing to listen.

She had insisted the toe movements were nothing more than spasms. When I told her about the power returning to my legs, she said that was probably just spasms too.

'You lift up my leg and I'll show you,' I said.

Up went the leg.

'I will push . . . now,' I said.

Feeling was believing. Jacquie conceded I had made a voluntary leg movement. For the first time, a health professional had given me the benefit of the doubt.

Jacquie organised a couple of pulleys to be installed over my bed so I could work on building up my triceps. The weights on the pulleys were only one kilogram, but even with the support of my arm braces I struggled to get the pulleys to the end of the cord. I found that hard to take. As a 52-kilo jockey, I had been able to throw a 50-kilo bag of oats around the stables, no worries.

Jacquie's encouragement was infectious. When she saw signs of improvement she urged me to do more. That's what I needed, what I had always thrived on—achieving a goal and then being challenged to achieve even more. The doctors seemed paranoid about giving any positive feedback for fear of offering false hope. Even Jacquie never mentioned the 'w' word—walking—but at least she encouraged me to make whatever improvement I could as soon as I could.

I was also going to the gym for workouts most days. The doctors had decided I was ready to move out of 13 EW to the Austin's specialist rehabilitation centre at Kew, the Royal Talbot.

The way people at 13 EW talked about the Talbot made it sound like paradise.

'You think the food's good here,' they would say, 'well, you just wait until you go to the Talbot. It's like a five-star hotel.'

At the Talbot you could get a double bed in a room with its own toilet and shower. The beds were lovely and soft. The rehabilitation program was better than the Austin's gym, they said. I couldn't wait to get there.

The head physiotherapist at the Austin, Yvonne Duncan, sensed my need for positive reinforcement. On the eve of leaving for the Talbot, I'd just finished my gym workout when Yvonne stood in front of my wheelchair, leaned over and put her arms around me. This was no mere goodbye hug. She pulled me up out of my seat, locking her knees to mine to support me. Suddenly I was on my feet. It felt wonderful to be upright again, even though my legs felt like dead weights. I dropped my head onto Yvonne's shoulder and burst into tears.

Charity from
home

13

The thoroughbred fraternity can be as quick as any to rip down its tall poppies. Fortunately, most people in the business respect those who have made it to the top by their own hard work and are more than willing to lend a hand when a mate hits hard times.

The support I got from the racing industry, especially from Tasmania, was overwhelming. From the day of my fall I had cards and letters flowing in with messages of sympathy and support. There were cards from Japan, England and America. Lester Piggott, Britain's greatest jockey, who I'd ridden against on one of his guest appearances in Australia, sent his best wishes. The top American rider Kent Desormeaux, who had overcome a serious head injury in 1992, sent a photograph of his win in that year's Kentucky Derby with the message: 'Never give up. Dreams do come true. You have to strive, chase, fight, do what it takes to achieve them.'

Darren Bennett, the Australian Rules footballer who had successfully transferred to gridiron in the United States, sent this one: 'Success is not luck, it's a personality trait. You've already proved it once and this time is no different.'

Among the dozens of cards pinned on a board next to my bed at the Austin intensive care unit, one of the most special was a huge card with dozens of messages from racing people, collected by the racing radio station in Melbourne, 3UZ.

Within a fortnight of my fall, the Tasmanian racing industry had organised a public fundraising appeal under the chairmanship of Michael Hodgman.

The only money I had to rely on was a personal insurance policy, which paid out $600 a week for up to two years, or a lump sum. That wasn't going to cover the costs of converting our house to be wheelchair-friendly, let alone pay for things like physiotherapy and medication, which, at that stage, looked like being permanent requirements.

The Mercury newspaper, the TAB, Purity supermarkets, Roelf Vos stores and the Commonwealth and Trust banks all made their branches available for taking donations. The public response was amazing—$75 000 in the first month.

Tanya Coward, a friend who had worked as a strapper for a few stables, put together a fundraiser at Spreyton racecourse that boosted the pool. Damien Oliver was kind enough to sign a set of riding boots for auction.

Jamie Evans, a jumps jockey who had suffered serious injuries himself in race falls, did a lot of work behind the scenes.

Tasmania's Seven Network affiliate, Southern Cross Television, got behind the appeal with a telethon on 11 July.

A lot of very busy people—sports and TV personalities—gave their time to help out. But the general public of Tasmania were the real stars with their generosity, pledging more than $80 000 through the telethon.

As well as the phone lines being staffed at the Southern Cross studio, there was a function at Wrest Point casino the same night as the telethon. It was organised by Barry Larter, one of the most prominent racehorse owners and breeders in Tassie. I had ridden lots of big winners for him, including the Tassie two-year-old champion, Alfa. He owned Vaudeville Piper and really appreciated what I had done for 'Vaudey' in the float accident that had killed some of his other horses.

Who says bookmakers don't have a heart? The first donation announced on the live Southern Cross broadcast was $1000 from the Tasmanian Bookmakers Association. The TV vet Dr Harry Cooper, Ronnie Burns and Lyn Talbot from 'Healthy Wealthy and Wise', and several other Channel Seven personalities put in appearances on the broadcast.

The bidding for some of the donated auction items showed how loyal Tasmanians are to their own. A signed guernsey from Garry Lyon, of the Melbourne AFL team, fetched $450. Nathan Buckley's signed Collingwood jumper raised $650, and the North Melbourne jumper carrying Wayne Carey's autograph made $950. While these were among the biggest names in Australian football, none of them had that home-town Tassie appeal. On the other hand, the overalls donated by Devonport car racing ace John Bowe sold for $1300, and the axe of world champion wood chopper David Foster went for $3000. Shane Warne's signed Australian cricket team top attracted a top bid of $750, less than half the $2200 put up for a bat presented by Tassie's star batsman, Ricky Ponting.

Darren Beadman, the well-known jockey who had quit race riding at the peak of his career to pursue his Christian faith with community work, came down from Sydney to help not only with the telethon but with a fundraiser at Mowbray to be held the following day by the Tasmanian Turf Club.

My biggest rival on the Tassie jockey's circuit, Stephen Maskiell, also attended the telethon phones.

I had been at the Talbot just over a week when the telethon went to air, and those first few days had been a nightmare. On telethon night, Southern Cross organised a live cross from their studio to the Talbot for a short interview with Mum and me.

The host, Neil Kearney, asked me how things were going and what my hopes were for the future.

'I just want to come home, to be honest,' I said.

I thanked everybody in Tassie for their support and told them how much it had helped keep my chin up, but I had to admit there had been times when I'd been terribly depressed.

I thought I'd got through the interview without letting my guard down, but then I sent out a message to Dad, who was watching the live telecast from the casino function. My voice cracked and the tears started to flow as I said hello and that 'I just want to say I love him'.

Later that month, the Tasmanian Carbine Club organised another big fundraiser, a 400-guest affair at the Hotel Grand Chancellor in Hobart with Gai Waterhouse as the featured speaker. Gai called me at the Talbot on her way to the airport that morning. Although we had quite a bit in common as women who had had to fight to be recognised in the racing industry, we hardly knew each other personally. She was easy to talk to, and by the end of the conversation I found myself having a dig at her for not using women riders.

Unfortunately all this generosity directed at me led to some disgruntlement among disabled people and their families, with some complaining that I was getting special treatment because of my high profile, while lots of other quadriplegics, many of them worse off than I was, were getting nothing. When the appeal closed I made it known that anyone wanting to make a donation in future should send it to their local quadriplegics' association.

I couldn't believe that so many people I had never heard of would come out of the woodwork to give their time and money.

There are too many to name individually, but Gary Grant— 'Gee-Gee' to his mates—was one of the people who weren't even racing followers yet came forward to help anyway. From the first television news reports of the fall, something pricked Gary's interest and he felt a strong need to help.

He contacted Honda about their four-wheel motorbikes and they sent their Melbourne sales manager to Tassie to see Mum and Dad and find out exactly what I'd need.

Honda offered to supply the vehicle at cost price.

To raise the money to pay for it, Gary organised a function at Moonee Valley racecourse through the Victorian Thoroughbred Club. There were no Gai Waterhouses or Darren Beadmans at Gary's fundraiser, just ordinary people giving their time and money. Someone from the Morwell Football Club had heard a radio ad for a raffle Gary had organised and rang him to volunteer to sell tickets. A couple of weeks later, having sold all the tickets, he rang back for more. In the end the footy club crew from Morwell, a town of 14 000 people 150 kilometres east of Melbourne, sold hundreds of tickets, more than anyone else.

About 200 people turned out at Moonee Valley, and at the end of the night Gary had raised half the money for the four-wheel motorbike.

A few weeks after I had returned home from the Talbot, Gary had Honda fly the motorbike to Tasmania and he came over to deliver it personally.

'Why are you doing this?' I asked him.

'Because . . .' was all he could offer.

Before my accident I'd been inspired by my parents' hard work and willingness to keep chasing their dreams even when the breaks went against them. After the fall I found out what real hardship was all about. It wasn't the loss of material things—what mattered was your health and having friends and loved ones you could rely on. I discovered that the Aussie spirit of helping out someone in less fortunate circumstances was alive and well.

There weren't too many good things that came out of my accident, but I will always treasure the pure human kindness of all the people who gave from their hearts and wallets.

To all the above, and the dozens I don't have room to mention, thank you all very, very much.

Tough love

14

The Royal Talbot rehabilitation centre certainly has a five-star location, set amid native bushland overlooking the Yarra River in the upmarket inner-eastern Melbourne suburb of Kew.

The ambulance that took me there on a cold winter Saturday in early July 1998 snaked its way along the riverside road, past joggers and cyclists taking in the view and die-hard golfers making an early start on the Yarra Bend course.

From the main entrance, on the high ground of the north bank of the river, you could look back to the skyline of gleaming office towers in the central city. Although it enjoyed a prime position, the Talbot's buildings were humble, a series of low, chocolate-brown brick villas, like those you might find in an outer suburban public housing development.

I was taken by wheelchair to my new home, a large room that had wardrobes, cupboards and two beds, which made it feel less like a hospital ward.

My room-mate was a 16-year-old quadriplegic boy who had gone over the handlebars of his BMX bike.

I took a quick tour of the main building, which was separated into accommodation for paraplegics on one side and quadriplegics on the other. There was a communal cafeteria where all the patients and their families and visitors had their meals.

It was worth getting to know the ladies who worked in the cafeteria—you always seemed to get a better meal from the ones you got on with personally. The rule was that patients ate for free, but relatives had to pay. One of the ladies, a fellow owner of cocker spaniels, would slip Mum a meal at no charge when she could.

While the Talbot's physical set-up was much more like the outside world than the Austin's had been, the social environment was quite unnerving. In 13 EW I got to know John and some of the others well enough to share a laugh or private thoughts. Here everyone seemed to have withdrawn into their own little world.

My teenaged room-mate hardly said anything to me, and I didn't really know what to say to him either. Later on Sam, a girl who had been in 13 EW at the Austin, moved in with me and that was a lot better.

It soon became apparent that the division between the 'paras' and 'quads' went deeper than the fact that we slept in different wings. As a new patient, I got the once-over from each set of eyes I wheeled past. Within a few seconds they had you summed up.

The first and easiest check they made was to see if you

were a complete 'quad', only able to move your head. In that case, you would be using a motorised wheelchair, pressing your chin onto a control pad. The second glance went to your hands: 'paras' could grip the wheel of their chair with their fingers; 'incomplete quads' could only push with the heel of their palms. The big one was your legs. Once they saw I could lift my feet off the footrest, I was labelled a 'walker'. Perhaps I was paranoid, but those who didn't have my level of movement didn't seem to want to know me after they saw that.

The return of feeling and movement in my legs was a double-edged sword. That first night at the Talbot my legs felt as if they were on fire. The bed was as rock hard as any in the Austin. I hardly had a minute's sleep and my groaning was loud enough to disturb my room-mate. The nurses gave me aspirin for the pain but it didn't have much effect— every muscle in my legs seemed to be locked in a bad cramp.

Because it was the weekend there was no doctor on duty. Mum and Kim were staying at the flat at the Austin and when Mum came in to visit she went around pleading for a doctor until eventually one was called in. He gave me Panadeine Forte, which took the edge off the pain but still couldn't get me off to sleep.

In the morning I was introduced to the new method of getting me out of bed until I learned how to do it for myself. Nurses weren't allowed to turn patients over during the night or lift them out of bed in the morning because of the risk of injuring their backs. So I had to wait for the turners to get me up. They used a hoist, which hauled the upper body up using straps around the backside and shoulders. The turners lifted a leg each, which had the unfortunate effect of pulling my legs apart and making me lose my bowel control. This was not a very encouraging start to my day.

Later that morning it got even worse. I fell into a panic attack in the toilet and almost passed out. The fear factor was getting the better of me again. I was scared of turning off the light at night because of the long hours of sleepless pain in the dark that lay ahead. For the next few days I was in a high state of anxiety every time I went into the bathroom for fear of going into a mental meltdown. To overcome my fear I had to make short visits during the day, just sitting there in my wheelchair without going to the toilet, to rebuild my confidence in being able to get in and out with my nerves under control.

The leg pain wouldn't go away. I was taking more and more Panadeine Forte, more than I was prescribed, but it wasn't working. Sometimes I was calling the nurses every twenty minutes through the night. They gave me massages and stretches, the turners rolled me into different positions, but it made no difference.

For a quadriplegic, there is one thing worse than having pain—having no pain. Finally, because of my constant calls for help overnight and the amount of Panadeine Forte I was chewing through, I was given an indocid suppository, an anti-inflammatory treatment that works by dissolving after being inserted in your rectum. Yes, it sounds unpleasant but I was in so much distress I was willing to try anything.

It took away the pain, all right. Not only the pain, but

all the sensation in my legs as well. That really frightened me. What if I'd lost all the feeling I'd recovered over the past six weeks? Were these the only two choices I had—unbearable pain or total numbness? If this was the five-star life, God help me.

The next few weeks took me to the lowest point of my life.

I had had such high hopes and expectations of how quickly I would progress at the Talbot that the reality was a real letdown. The first controlled movement of my hands had come quickly after that first wiggle of my toe, but progress from then on was frustratingly slow. I was still basically a wind-up doll with a flat battery.

I didn't want anyone outside the family and my closest friends, Kim Dixon and Dianne Parish, to see me like this. I gave the front desk a standing instruction not to let through any visitors who hadn't been approved in advance. One day Gary Willetts, the Kiwi jockey who moved to Australia to become one of the top riders of the '80s, came in. He had taken a strong interest in jockeys' welfare after retiring and wanted to bring Scobie Breasley, the legendary Melbourne and Caulfield Cups winning rider of the 1940s and '50s to visit me. 'Sorry,' said the person on the front desk, 'you're not on the list.'

I felt so embarrassed about my condition that I withdrew from contact with people as far as possible. Some of the other Talbot patients would come into my room for a chat, but I would only offer enough conversation to be polite.

On weekends the staff organised outings to the city. The 'paras' and 'quads' piled their wheelchairs into vans and went off to join the real world, feeding ducks in the park or having lunch at a café. Not me. I got out of it by saying I had promised Dad my first outing into town would be with him.

I became good at making excuses. I became pretty demanding, too. I suppose this was my way of regaining some self-esteem. Having been in charge of my life for so long, to suddenly be reliant on others just to get out of bed or go to the toilet was devastating. Getting my own way on petty things made me feel I still had some control.

Everyone was desperate to make me happy, so I had no trouble getting anything I demanded from my loved ones. I got into comfort eating—Maltesers, Tim Tams, ice cream, chips . . . When Dad, Jason, and Kim came to visit they would bring me a mountain of sweets. The three of them would stay by my side from the moment I got up until I went to bed. If I wanted a drink, a massage or a push around the grounds in my wheelchair all I had to do was ask.

Mum says I was like a six-year-old child, craving attention and testing the limits of what I could get away with. She loved me just as much as the others, but she didn't think giving in to this behaviour was good for me in the long term. Eventually I would have to come out into the real world where there would be no roster of servants to grant me my every whim.

Mum decided the best love she could give me was tough love. When she wanted to go to the cafeteria for a cup of coffee and I turned on the tears and pleaded, 'Please, Mum, stay with me,' she would get up and say: 'I'm just going for a coffee, Bev. I'll be back in a few minutes.'

If I asked her to go and get me some junk food after I'd finished my visitors' supply, she would say, 'No, you've had enough of that rubbish. You're putting on far too much weight.'

When she discovered I'd been taking extra, unauthorised painkillers, she dobbed me in to the nurse. I got a lecture about the importance of them knowing what medication I was having in case they gave me something that caused an adverse reaction—the tablets I had been raiding from my bedside drawer didn't mix well with aspirin, for instance.

Another time I was complaining about how hard my bed was and how I'd been told I'd get a nice, soft double bed when I moved to the Talbot from the Austin. Mum said she would find out about a bigger bed. When she came back, she said she had tried one out and that it was twice as hard as the one I had. 'You're so lucky to have this one,' she said. 'You want to hang on to this as long as you can.' Of course, she was making it up, but it stopped me feeling so hard done by.

It was a very tough time for Mum, who was the one who spent most time with me at the Talbot. She was distressed by how my condition was getting the better of me mentally. The social worker's notes at the end of my first week at Kew picked this up: 'Bev's mother has been reacting very emotionally to Bev's distress and anxiety . . . encouraged mother to look at overall improvement, to see Bev's grieving as a positive event and put limits on Bev's demands. She noted Bev responds to firm direction when tearful and upset.'

When the social worker was not around I often responded to Mum's 'firm direction' with some 'firm directions' of my own. We had some terrible arguments and it must have taken all Mum's strength to stick to her guns. She would tell Dad, Kim and Jason not to do everything for me, but they said they just wanted to make me happy. Mum knew me better, though. 'Bev will only be happy,' she said, 'when she can do things for herself.' As much as I wouldn't admit it then, she was dead right.

I withdrew further and further into my own little world.

Although I was depressed, I refused to see the psychologist. She wasn't going to be any use in helping me walk again, I told myself, and besides, she had more than her hands full with everyone else's problems.

Not long after my move to the Talbot, I had a dream that I had got up out of my wheelchair, started walking and then broken into a run. It was very vivid so when I woke up and found myself still a cripple it made me very upset. I felt as if I was being tortured mentally as well as physically.

I got so bad that at one point I started to think that my injuries were punishment for having felt awkward around disabled people before my fall. I'd been so fit and had enjoyed the physical, outdoor life so much that when I had come into contact with disabled people, I felt awful about how much they were missing out on. So much so that I felt uncomfortable around them. Now God was teaching me a lesson.

I wished the world would go away and forget about Bev Buckingham, but fortunately it wouldn't. Although I had shunned all but my closest family and friends, people I had never even met were out there trying to help.

Darren Bennett, the AFL footballer who had made it into

the big time of American football with the San Diego Chargers, heard about the fundraising effort being undertaken by the Tasmanian racing industry. He contacted some American sports stars to get them to sign some of their sporting memorabilia to send over for fundraiser auctions.

Then he had a better idea. He got in touch with Christopher Reeve through Scott Yoffe, the public relations officer for the Chargers, and told him about my accident. As a result of that, a two-page letter from the famous actor arrived at the Royal Talbot in early August. Here's my letter from Superman:

Dear Bev,

There are no words to describe how profoundly I can identify with your present situation. Many spinal cord injuries happen to people who fall off ladders or are involved in automobile accidents. Those incidents are horrific in their own right, but as you and I both know, to be injured while participating in our favourite sport, aboard an animal we have loved and cared for, is particularly devastating.

The equestrian community around the world joins me in sending you our deepest sympathy. But this letter is not meant to convey only a message of commiseration. As president of the American Paralysis Association, which provides funding to leading spinal cord researchers around the world, I am grateful to be able to send you words of real encouragement and hope. The secret of regeneration in the spinal cord has now been discovered and human trials are not far off. The ancient wisdom that the broken cord cannot be repaired is now as outdated as the concept that the world is flat.

Many scientists now believe that making the appropriate reconnections across the injury site and its surrounding scar tissue will not be as difficult as it once seemed to be. There is even evidence that the spinal cord has a memory and under certain circumstances motor function can be created without input from the brain. This seems to support the theory that once the reconnections are made, whether through cell transplants, nerve grafts, gene therapy, the introduction of antibodies or a 'cocktail' of all of the above, a healthy body has an excellent chance of recovery.

I hope this benefit [an upcoming fundraiser] brings you the funds you need to endure your present situation. But be proactive, challenge yourself physically and know that a positive attitude and belief in recovery can no longer be considered wishful thinking. They are all keys to your future.

On behalf of hundreds of thousands of people living with paralysis today, I send you my very best wishes.

Sincerely,
Christopher Reeve

I felt humbled that such a famous international star would take the time to write to me. It would be nice to say that his words instantly inspired me out of my black mood and repaired my broken spirit, but it was not that simple. It would take time, more tough love and a move away from the Talbot to do that.

There is a basic routine for training horses. Long, slow work to get them fit, followed by building up the sprint at the end of their gallops until they are going at full pace for the last 800 or 1000 metres, as they would in a race. Good trainers know that no two horses are the same. They vary the routine to suit the individual horse. If you have one that has put on too much weight in the 'spelling' paddock, you stick with the slow work until it has burned off the excess fat. A 'clean-winded' horse that has a more efficient lung capacity than average won't need many fast gallops to reach race fitness.

The thing that disappointed me about the rehabilitation program at the Talbot was the 'one size fits all' approach. Each week I had a schedule pinned up next to my bed that laid out my daily routine of physiotherapy, occupational therapy and gym sessions. When I got to the appointment the staff member would give me the standard workout and off I would go to my next routine.

At the Austin, I had my most productive sessions under Jacquie, who, like a good trainer, jumped to the next level when she saw I was making progress and tried to think of new ways to help me advance when the improvement levelled off.

It's not that the staff at the Talbot weren't doing their best. This was the era when Victoria's hospitals were having to cope with big budget and staff cuts and there were just too few qualified people to give each patient individual attention all the time. The result was that someone like me, whose body was recovering and was ready to cope with an accelerated program, had to fit into the same schedule as everyone else.

One of the first things I had to learn was how to roll over. Until I could do this, I wouldn't get the double bed I fantasised would be the answer to a restful night's sleep. The turners couldn't reach a patient properly to roll them over on a double bed, so you had to prove you could do it for yourself before you could have one.

To learn to roll, you start by lying on a mattress on the floor. The basic idea is to turn your top half first to create momentum for your legs to follow. It took me three weeks to get enough strength and coordination into my turns to go through the night with no assistance.

The next thing I had to learn was how to get myself in and out of the wheelchair. The key to this is using a slide-board, which functions as a cross between a bridge and a see-saw, to get you between your wheelchair and the bed. It requires a lot of upper body strength and my gym sessions weren't getting me where I needed to be as quickly as I wanted. I began my own strength training in bed by reaching back onto the head board and pulling up the dead weight of my body. I insisted that side rails were put up around my bed every night so I could use them to lever myself into different positions without having to wait for the turners.

This was the sort of extra workload I wanted the medical staff to suggest. But it never came. The standing frame exercise was another example of this. It was used to help me regain my sense of balance and build up my legs to take my body weight again. My knees were locked into position to stop me falling forward and a strap around my backside held me in to the standing frame from behind. At the start I could only take my weight for a few minutes, but each day I improved.

I was telling Dad about it on the phone one night—how I was lasting longer and longer on the standing frame.

'You should try lifting your legs as if you were walking,' he said. I hadn't thought that possible and nor had my physiotherapist. When I started trying it, I soon found I could get one foot at a time a few centimetres off the ground.

There were times, though, when my impatience got the better of me. Dianne Parish was up for a visit after I had been on the standing frame for less than two weeks. She stayed with me for a week, allowing Mum to go home for a rest. Like Kim, Dianne was always there when I needed her, and she was always so bubbly and funny I couldn't help but have a laugh when she was at my bedside. Later I learned Di shed her share of tears for me, but she never let me see that she was hurting when she was 'on duty'.

I told Di I had mastered the slideboard and was ready to try getting from the wheelchair into bed without it. I asked her to help support me. Di was still riding then and weighed around 50 kilos. With my new comfort food diet I had shot up to almost 60 kilos and poor Di couldn't take my weight. My legs gave way and we both sank to the floor in slow motion. It took about half an hour to find someone to come and lift me off the floor.

I had another scare at the hydrotherapy pool. For my first session I was fitted with 'floaties', the inflatable supports children wear when they are learning to swim. I hadn't been in the water very long when my muscles went into spasm. Usually I was able to control my spasms, but this time I just couldn't stop them and with my head immersed in water, and my body trussed up in floaties, I was panic-stricken. The staff had to carry me to the edge of the pool and lift me out. My body felt like such a huge dead weight as they hauled me out of the water. I vowed I'd never get back in that pool again.

Dad and I made a secret pact. As soon as he could get our house modified for me, I'd come home and do my own recovery program our way. He worked out that 12 August was the earliest date he could have the design finished, clear all the council permits and get tradesmen in to do the work.

Losing the routine I had lived by most of my life—up at dawn for trackwork, feeding the horses, off to the races—left me feeling cut off from the real world. I needed to get back to Brigadoon, back with the horses, to even start regaining any sense of normality.

I told the medical team straight out: I was leaving on 11 August, so they had better have me ready. That seemed to put a bit more urgency into them—the usual rehab program lasted about twelve weeks, I was giving them six.

I continued to get tripped up by racing ahead of my capabilities. One night Jason was about to leave to go home and I said I would see him out to the car. I wheeled myself down the ramp to the carpark and waved him off. When I turned around to go back inside, I found I wasn't strong enough to wheel myself back up the ramp. It was getting close to 8 p.m. and I was wondering what time they locked the doors—

I didn't fancy spending all night out in the carpark. I sat there wondering what to do. One answer was to take a bit of a run-up—or roll-up—so that by the time I got to the ramp I would have enough speed to carry me up the slope and through the doors. But I was worried I might end up going too fast. The sliding doors opened automatically from a sensor triggered as you approached them. If I went over the sensor too quickly, the doors wouldn't have time to open and I would bounce back off the glass. Finally, after a bit of experimentation, I found I could get more leverage on my wheels if I went up backwards. Moral of the story: more weights work required in the gym and more practice on ramps.

The next challenge was learning to go up steps. This required lifting the front of the wheelchair off the ground and onto the step above, then pushing the back wheels up with sheer strength. It's a tricky manoeuvre. When you are learning it you start by doing 'wheelstands' in your chair, balancing on the back wheels with the front ones in the air as if you are placing them on a step. You have someone behind you to catch you if the wheelchair goes over backwards. The first time I tried it the student who was responsible for catching me wasn't paying attention. When I tipped over backwards I crashed straight to the ground, getting an awful fright and a solid whack on the head.

The next time I tried it I went over backwards again and was caught just before I hit the ground. I just had to grit my teeth and tell myself that graduating from the climbing steps class would take me that bit closer to being able to go home.

By early August, after a month at the Talbot, I was using the slideboard well enough to get myself between the wheelchair and the bed. Doing activities such as woodwork had improved the flexibility of my hands, and Jason's parents had brought over some squeezy toys to work on in my own time. As a result, with the aid of implement holders, I became able to comb my hair and use a toothbrush and eat with a knife and fork. For these tasks I wore what is called a 'palmar pocket' on my right hand, which was more impaired than my left even though I was naturally right-handed. The palmar pocket was strapped around the palm of the hand with Velcro straps. It had a pocket attachment that fitted into the cup of the hand, which could be adjusted to different angles. I used the pocket to hold my toothbrush, my knife or comb, which would otherwise have fallen to the ground from my weak grip.

Despite my progress, the medical people still hammered the point that I shouldn't expect miracles. My physiotherapist told me that even if I got back on my feet, I would need crutches or some other walking aid and that I would definitely never run.

My instant reaction was to think, 'You want to bet on it? I'll show you. I'll run again.'

Just having that thought was another boost. My old guts and determination was coming back.

The week before I was due to leave the Talbot, I was transferred to a special flat, set up to test whether I was ready for the outside world.

Kim came over and we had a ball together. We slept in a double bed and Kim would help me whenever I had trouble with my turns. The idea was to have me doing everything from taking a shower to cooking meals. We made pizzas on the special low kitchen benches designed for people in wheel-chairs. One morning, sitting on the commode having my shower, I decided to have a go at standing up. I pushed myself up with my arms until I could take all the weight on my legs. This was the first time I had stood up without the support of a standing frame. Oh, what a feeling!

This called for a celebration. That afternoon Kim went out and bought a bottle of vodka and some cigarettes—she'd tried to adhere to the no-smoking rules in these units, but the excitement of the occasion was too much. We put on some music and got nice and tipsy. Soon we were giggling just like the old days when we were teenage apprentices. I hadn't felt so normal for a long, long time.

I rang up one of the nurses to ask if they wanted to come over for a farewell drink.

'You know we do not allow alcohol on the premises,' she replied.

That was the official line, but she obviously didn't work into the wee hours when the 'paras' had their parties.

The trial in the flat went without a hitch, and when I woke up on 11 August it was as if my life was about to begin again. I had missed Tassie terribly. The family had been with me for the whole time in Melbourne, but only in shifts, never all together in our own space. Today we would all be together for the first time since my fall three months before.

The Tasmanian Government, which owned the Spirit of Tasmania car and passenger ferry that ran between Melbourne and the island, had organised a special homecoming voyage.

The Premier, Tony Rundle, would be at the head of the welcoming committee when we pulled into Devonport. I was so excited when the Spirit pulled away from the Port of Melbourne docks. At last I was on my way home.

One of the luxury suites on the Spirit had been named in my honour and the government gave it to us for free for the journey home. There was only one hitch: my wheelchair wouldn't fit through the door of the Beverley Buckingham Suite, so I had to spend the overnight journey in a wheelchair-friendly room. It didn't bother me in the slightest. The next day I would be back at Brigadoon. There, with my family around me, I could get my head and my body back into shape.

The next morning at the Devonport waterfront, Dad and Jason wheeled me into a press conference before we set off for home. Being on Tassie soil again, being back together as a family, made it a very emotional morning. Jason broke down and cried—the first time I'd seen him dissolve in tears since the accident. He'd been the one who had handled it best, never seeming to let things get him down or to doubt I'd make a full recovery.

'It's a miracle,' he told the reporters, before his voice cracked and he started sobbing. I leaned over and pulled him in to cry on my shoulder. I had missed him so much when I was in hospital and it was great to think we were about to start rebuilding out life together.

Inevitably one journalist asked the 'Will you walk again?' question.

'I will never give up, even if it takes ten years,' I said. 'I will never accept how I am.'

One step at a time

15

Home, sweet home.

As soon as we pulled up at the front gate of Brigadoon, with the horses mooching around in their paddocks and the crisp air disturbed only by the birds, I felt I was back to reality.

While the feel of the place was just as I remembered, the look of the house was another matter. I hardly recognised it. For three weeks carpenters, electricians and plumbers had been changing everything from the width of the doorways to the handles on the taps.

Jason's and my bedroom had been converted into a mini rehabilitation ward. Dad had had a wall knocked down to extend the room to hold a 2-metre massage table and a standing frame. A sliding door led to a new balcony so I could take a break outside without having to wheel myself right through the house.

The biggest job was the new en suite bathroom. Everything had to be ripped out and rebuilt from scratch. I needed a vanity unit that was not only lower than normal but had nothing below the bench in the middle so I could roll my wheelchair underneath. Standard hot and cold tap handles that required gripping and turning were unworkable for me. I had to have levers. The water system had to be temperature-controlled because I couldn't fine tune the mixture of hot and cold. The toilet had a specially padded commode—the ones I had used in Melbourne were so hard that after a few minutes they gave me a sore backside.

It was a wonderful feeling to sleep in my own bed again next to my husband. Jason would help me turn during the night and in the morning he'd assist me into the shower, onto the toilet and with the fiddlier bits of getting dressed.

The hallway from the bedroom to the rest of the house was wide enough for a wheelchair but the doorways were not. They all had to be widened and the internal doors removed. The whole house had to have ducted heating set at a constant temperature because my internal thermometer was still faulty. If I was in a room at a normal temperature of about 20 degrees Celsius and you wheeled me into a meat coolstore in a T-shirt it would take 10 minutes before I started to feel chilly. Then, once it hit me that I was cold, you could take me back into the 20-degree room and it would take half an hour before my teeth stopped chattering.

Because of this our heating and cooling bills ran into the hundreds each month. Without my insurance payout, which I took as a lump sum, and the fundraising appeal, which

reached $200 000, we would not have been able to afford
the renovating and running costs at Brigadoon.

Last but not least were the wheelchair ramps at the front
and back entrances to the house. The kitchen didn't need
changing because we had always had a neat division of labour
in our household. I worked ten hours a day outside feeding
horses, mucking out their boxes, riding them in trackwork
and checking on those out in the paddocks. If there was a
fence that needed repairing or a drain that needed digging,
I just rolled up my sleeves and did it. Inside, Mum did all
the cooking, cleaning and washing. I certainly wasn't in any
shape to start playing the domestic goddess now.

Being at home took away a lot of the stress factors I
experienced at the Talbot. I was at home with my family
now, among people I knew inside out and who knew me
the same way—no more feeling like I was under scrutiny
every time I went into a room among other patients. Here
I could set my own routine and didn't have to slot into
someone else's hour-by-hour schedule.

It was surprising, then, that a couple of weeks after I got
home my hair started to fall out. Not just a few strands when
I brushed it, but big clumps. When I left the Talbot I had a
nice thick head of dark brunette hair down past my shoulders.
A month later I could hardly muster a respectable pony tail.

Perhaps it was my body reacting to new stresses. When I
was in the Talbot, dreaming about coming home, the most
burning desire was to be back with my horses. But from the
first day I got home I found I couldn't muster the courage
to go outside and get close to them. I suppose it's a bit like

when you're a teenager and you become besotted with a boy. You daydream all day about being with him, but the minute he enters the room you just want to hide in the corner. I loved my horses so much—I loved *riding* them so much— that I couldn't face them.

Mum and Dad didn't force the issue, but every now and then Dad would offer to take me outside for a stable visit. Finally, after a couple of weeks, I worked up the nerve to confront my heart-throbs. I hated being stuck down in the wheelchair, having to look up into their eyes knowing our relationship was never going to be as close as before. Some horses seemed frightened of the wheelchair and backed away.

For the next few weeks I stayed away from the stables. Mum and Dad couldn't believe it. I'd talked for weeks in the Talbot about how desperate I was to see my pets and how they would bring me back to the land of the living, but in those early weeks I was still floating in psychological and emotional outer space.

As time went on, I began getting out on a three-wheel electric scooter to feed the horses. I'd drive the scooter out to the horse boxes, open the doors, pick up the water buckets, fill them up and put them back in the stall. That felt a little bit more normal, like I was getting back to work again, and it was a weights and flexibility session at the same time. It made me feel there was light at the end of the tunnel.

The horses were still wary of me on the scooter and I couldn't relax around them—some of the nervier ones could get spooked and bowl me over, scooter and all, at any minute.

There was one special horse I could bank on, though. Gary was munching his retirement days away in a paddock about a kilometre from the house. I asked Dad to wheel me up to see him—I knew he could make me feel relaxed and safe around horses again.

From the muddy laneway leading to his paddock, I could see him in the distance. As soon as he saw me his ears pricked up. When Dad opened the gate, the sight of me in a wheelchair didn't spook him at all. I didn't even have to call him. The big stallion strolled over, craned his magnificent head down into my shoulder and nibbled a kiss on my neck. That was my Gary, as strong as a bull and as gentle as a puppy.

'That's my boy,' I said, as I rubbed his muzzle and kissed him back.

I stroked his neck and remembered our glory days together. On the track he had given me total confidence, and now was no different. He stood there quietly for ten or fifteen minutes with the same unconditional trust in me, even though he hadn't seen me for months.

Now I felt I had truly arrived home.

When I left the Talbot the doctors wanted me to complete my rehab through the Launceston Hospital. With no disrespect to the staff there, I had had enough of medical institutions. I wanted people who could work with me one-on-one, at my pace. It would cost a lot more but I knew it would be worth it.

A district nurse had come out to see Mum at Brigadoon to advise on things I would need when I came home. Mum asked if there were any physiotherapists the nurse could recommend.

'I know a fantastic one,' the nurse said. 'We're very lucky to have her here in Tasmania. Her name is Naami Brown.'

Mum rang Naami, whose practice was at Ulverston, ten minutes' drive away. Naami asked Mum all about me and arranged to come and see her to talk about what we had in mind. At that first meeting, Mum stressed I needed to be encouraged and challenged.

'The more you drive her, the more she will try for you,' Mum said. 'Don't take no for an answer.'

In other words, more tough love.

I met Naami the day after I came home. I could tell from that first meeting that she was a lovely person and a true professional. She set out how she proposed to work with me five days a week, with a program of massage, stretches and exercises. Because her visits lasted for only an hour, she stressed that it was up to me to do the exercises she was teaching me in my own time. She also showed Jason, Mum and Kim how to do the massage and stretches so we could work on the flexibility of my joints in her absence.

For the first couple of days, the hour was taken up just with the massage and stretches—pushing my hands, knees, hips and wrists as far as they would go in each direction, keeping their machinery oiled for that magic day when the blockage in my spine, hopefully, would clear and the central nervous system engine would splutter back to life.

Naami was impressed that I had some movement in my knees, and by the end of the first week we were working on trying to get me up out of the wheelchair, with her supporting me rather than using the slideboard. After the massage and stretches, I stood in my frame, without my knees strapped in, and Naami asked me to take my weight on my legs for as long as I could. Then she got me to lift my feet off the ground one at a time, a creaky version of walking on the spot. She praised every effort I made and encouraged me to try harder.

After two weeks of Naami's treatment I decided to have a go at walking one night. Dad and Jason lifted me out of the chair and stood on either side of me. With my arms around their shoulders I could stay upright, but my legs couldn't take my weight and move at the same time. As I continued to make progress, Naami asked if I felt up to having another go. She'd be supporting me, holding me from behind around the hips if I crumpled.

'Let's do it,' I said.

Dad and Jason stood on either side and eased me off the frame. Naami held me around the waist. I stood there, like a diver on the high board, concentrating, building up the will to take that leap into thin air. I sucked in a deep breath and sent out the mental command for my right leg to take a step forward. I was as surprised and delighted as my audience when it obliged—hardly a step, more of a jerky shuffle. Before I knew it my left foot had crabbed forward to catch up.

'Come on legs, move,' I cried.

A few seconds passed. Then another right forward shuffle. Left forward shuffle. Right again, left again. The adrenaline was flowing. Dad, Jason and Naami cheered me on. Then suddenly my legs went to jelly. My slow motion momentum came to a halt and Dad and Jason guided me back into the chair.

We were all so excited it was hard to know what to think. Was this the big breakthrough, the turning point that would deliver me back to the world of the walking? Or just another side road that would come to a dead end?

Unlike the Talbot staff, Naami put her foot down on the accelerator rather than checking for the speed limit. After a few minutes getting my breath and strength back, she got me up for another try. Again, I managed to shuffle forward about two metres before I ran out of steam.

The next day I had another go. This time I went six metres. Six metres, the width of a bedroom. I'd travelled such a short distance, yet come so far.

Naami's next move was to get me on a 'gutter frame'. It's similar to a stationary standing frame but it has castors on the bottom to allow it to roll along while supporting the user. It's called a 'gutter frame' because it has two curved forearm rests—similar in shape to the guttering on a house—which point forward just above waist height for the user to lean on to support their weight.

This allowed me to extend my shuffle distances. By the end of the month I was going 50 metres at a time. I'd start in my exercise room, go out through the sliding door, along the verandah—ah, what a beautiful day—down the ramp, in the front door, down the hall and back to my room. My little band of followers—Naami, Mum, Dad and Jason—would trail along, with Naami's hands always ghosting my hips in case my legs gave way or tripped.

The quick progress from pretend walking in the standing frame to roaming around outside on the gutter frame made me glad we had forced the issue and taken control of my rehabilitation. I couldn't wait to get out of bed each day to see how much further I could get my legs to take me. Soon two metres had turned into 200—out onto the verandah, down the ramp, out to the front gate, back to the house, up the ramp and back inside.

By the middle of September, a month after coming home, I had graduated from the gutter frame to elbow crutches. These are shorter than conventional crutches and instead of tucking them under your armpit they have a smaller version of the 'gutter', which you use to support yourself by the elbows. Again, it was a matter of Naami teaching me the technique and supervising me on the new equipment, then relying on me to build up my leg strength and movement after she left.

In October we tackled going up and down steps. This was essentially a test of strength, first of the shoulders to haul my bodyweight up to the first step, then of the leg to hold it there while I lifted the other leg up. It was also a test of balance, and of my ability to overcome the fear of falling. I had flashbacks to the Austin and the head-cracking spill I took on my first try at climbing steps in a wheelchair.

Psychologically, the move to the arm crutches was as big a boost as taking that first shuffle-step. It was about as close as you could get to independent walking. The gutter frame was a long way from being in a wheelchair, but it was still an unwieldy contraption, obviously built for someone whose body couldn't perform a basic human function. The crutches took away the security blanket of wheels to help my legs move forward and a solid frame to hold my torso upright. With crutches, the upper body had to stand up for itself just as the legs did, otherwise I'd just topple forward. I would never walk properly unless I could get enough strength in my trunk to hold it straight.

Because my abdominal muscles had gone unused for so long, it was unclear whether they weren't working because of spinal damage or just lack of practice. Every now and then Naami would mention that she believed exercising in a swimming pool was a great way to work the stomach muscles, but after my experience at the Austin I wasn't ready to go back into the water.

It took until November for me to give in. By then Naami and I had built a very close working relationship, and the success her methods were having gave me the confidence that hydrotherapy was the next step I had to take.

Twice a week, for an hour, Naami hired the pool at the Latrobe rehabilitation centre for the two of us. In between spurts of walking against the resistance of the water, both forwards and backwards, and standing on one leg at a time, Naami would support me floating on my back. I would try to hold my torso straight using my stomach muscles.

As Christmas approached, Naami could see I was indeed going to walk again. The strength and flexibility was improving in my legs and abdomen all the time and every little increase in movement stimulated more muscle activity somewhere else. All I needed to do now was learn how to put it all together in one fluid motion instead of a series of clunky movements.

Even at my best, I was more staggering forward than walking. I tended to drag my feet flat along the ground.

I needed to consciously relearn the things you develop instinctively from childhood: placing your heel down first then rolling the foot forward and pushing off with the toe; swinging your left arm forward when the right leg goes forward and vice versa.

Although Naami hammered into me the need to keep up my homework—exercise-bike riding, weights, abdominal exercises—she made me take it easy before our appointments together so that the walking technique sessions were quality time. Despite the great progress I'd made, an hour session in the pool still left me drained, physically and mentally.

This was something people did not appreciate when the first media stories came out announcing that I was walking again. The papers made it sound as if I hopped out of bed each morning and strolled off down to the shops to buy the milk and bread. People thought I was 'cured'. They knew nothing about the 23 hours a day when I wasn't practising with my various walking aids: the muscle spasms triggered by pushing my legs harder than they were ready to go; the back pain that came with the increased sensation; the contortions required to move my bowels; not being able to hold a toothbrush; not being able to bend down to pat the dogs without toppling over.

Even so, in my own mind I was determined that I would get back to normal. By late December Naami felt she had done just about all she could. I was down to one arm-crutch, on my right arm, to support my right leg, which was quite a bit stiffer than the left. Jason came to a few pool sessions and Naami taught him how to support me through my exercise routine. Her Christmas present to me was to say I didn't need her any more.

On Christmas Day, Greg Richardson, who was as much a family friend as one of Dad's clients, came around for his usual Christmas visit. I hadn't seen him since he came to visit at the Royal Hobart the day after my fall. I'm not sure what he expected to find when he walked up the front ramp at Brigadoon on 25 December, seven months after he'd stood in front of the media explaining the extent of my spinal damage. From the tears that welled in his eyes, it was obvious he hadn't expected to find me opening the door, without a wheelchair or crutch in sight, saying, 'Hi Greg, come in.'

For the first six months back at Brigadoon I refused to go to the races. It was hard enough to go out the front door and see our horses in their paddocks, let alone witness them running—and especially winning—on race-day. That cut too close to the bone.

There was one engagement with the racing industry I couldn't avoid, though. A month after I got home I had to attend the stewards' inquiry into my fall. It was a trying day, not so much because of watching the fall in slow motion and putting my memory of it on the record, but because I had to sit in the same room with the other jockeys involved. They had all come out pretty much unscathed and it was uncomfortable for them, knowing they could just as easily have been the one in the wheelchair. I hated the idea of my old mates seeing me as a victim.

After watching the race film and hearing the evidence of all the riders, it was obvious it had just been one of those accidents that happen from time to time in such a risky sport as racing. It was plain bad luck I landed the way I did— a half-turn to one side or the other and I might have got away with a sore shoulder and a bit of concussion. The stewards found no one was to blame.

My next outing in the racing world gave me a taste of the practical difficulties of trying to have a social life as a quadriplegic. I accepted an invitation to the North-West Horse of the Year dinner at Spreyton racecourse. We were told to be there at 6 p.m. and we got there early. The dinner didn't start until 7.30. For the able-bodied, of course, the first 90 minutes was for catching up with other guests over a few pre-dinner drinks at the bar. For me, it was an hour-and-a-half spent catching a draught in my wheelchair. By the time the formalities got under way, my body was stiffening up, I was getting tired and felt like going home.

As the weeks went by, trainers and jockeys would drop in on their way to meetings at Spreyton to say hello and ask when I'd be back at the track. Race clubs had invited me, but I just wasn't ready to be reminded so pointedly that from now on when I went through the racecourse gates it would not be as a professional going to work but as another ex-jockey down on their luck. I was not going to make my return until I was out of the wheelchair.

Ironically, whenever those visitors asked what my long-term goal was, I didn't have to think twice before answering: 'Taking over the training from Dad.' To be a trainer you have to go to the races. I was going to have to face my racecourse demons sooner or later.

In the lead-up to Christmas I decided to ease myself back by going down to Spreyton late one morning on a non-race day. Dad drove me down and helped me into the three-wheeled scooter. Trackwork was winding down for the day. I wheeled past the stables where the last of the trainers and stable hands were packing up for the morning. They all smiled and called out that it was great to see me back. I tried to hold myself together but I felt so conspicuous and out of place in the scooter I burst into tears.

As my rehabilitation advanced I was more willing to get out and about in public. In January, when the big summer carnival was heating up, I accepted an invitation to a race-day function at Spreyton. Fortunately, the logistics meant I couldn't get too close to the horses or the atmosphere of the mounting yard. I was driven right up to the grandstand and helped up to the restaurant where the function was being held.

When Mum and I entered the room, I thought I'd made a breakthrough—spending more than five minutes at a race-course without crying. While I was coping OK, however, most of the rest of the guests weren't. I felt like the invisible woman. People seemed too embarrassed to come up and talk to me. I suppose they wanted to see the same old Bev they used to know.

I could understand how awkward these people felt—I'd been the same before I became the poor, unfortunate disabled person. Having been on both sides of the wheelchair, I think

I am qualified to offer this piece of advice on how to relate to 'paras' or 'quads': treat them like anyone else. As Mum once put it, they are normal people, only sitting down.

If it wasn't for the fact that Dad had a promising two-year-old lining up in one of the big races at the Hobart Cup carnival the following month, I don't know whether I would have bothered to go to Elwick in February. Again, I was at a special table at a restaurant function, but at least people seemed more at ease approaching me. By then I was getting around with just one hand-crutch, and having a few drinks certainly made me a bit more relaxed.

When the big two-year-old race came around, with our runner My Sienna the favourite, I had butterflies in my stomach, a sign the racing bug was regaining its grip on me. I shouted and screamed when My Sienna got locked on the rails in the straight. I felt cheated that she was beaten into third without getting a clear run. It made me so angry I had a bit to say about how she was ridden. That was a sign I was mentally getting back to something like my old self. Competitive, demanding, ready to go to war for my horse.

Around home I was feeling more confident and ready to get out and about. Although my beloved black Celica had manual gear change, I had good leg-and-arm control and I didn't see any reason why I shouldn't be able to drive. Apparently, 'paras' and 'quads' usually get their licence taken off them until they can show they are capable of driving or that they have modified their car to compensate for their disability. No paperwork had come through to me cancelling my licence, so one day I hopped in the car and drove over to Kim's place. She got the shock of her life when I pulled up and tooted to announce my arrival.

In May the Tasmanian TAB offered me a job as a public relations officer. Now that I was mobile it was just the sort of thing I needed to get back into the social life I'd enjoyed so much when I was riding. I went to openings of new TAB agencies with other Tasmanian sports stars, such as cricketer Ricky Ponting, and appeared in advertisements for big events on the racing calendar. For these appearances I had to have a bit of a makeover and some smart clothes, which all helped towards making me feel more confident in public.

My body had repaired itself about as much as it could; now it was time to get my psyche into shape to deal with life after being a jockey.

In March 1999, the Victorian Racing Media Association had voted me 'Personality of the Year' at their annual awards night. Although I appreciated the honour, I hadn't felt up to travelling to Melbourne to appear at such a big public occasion.

By July, with the TAB job under my belt, I felt more confident. When I received a call offering to fly Jason and me over to Melbourne for a belated presentation of the award I accepted.

We were taken to Flemington racecourse by Brian Meldrum, a Melbourne racing writer we got to know during my time in hospital in Melbourne.

It was a typically overcast Melbourne winter's day when we got to the course at about 10 a.m. There was no one there but us, a camera crew and a uniformed clerk of the course, on his grey horse, for the presentation ceremony on the lawn in front of the members' grandstand. Still, I never suspected for a second that this was a giant set-up until Mike Munro, the host of Channel Nine's 'This is Your Life', walked in to the fake award presentation with his big red book. I just broke up laughing, and, as I think the replay will show, jokingly threatened to throttle my husband. He'd kept a brilliant poker-face all the way through, as had Mum, Dad, Kim and the others, who at that moment were flying in to tape the show at Nine's studios in Richmond.

At the studio I was kept in a room on my own while all the guests went through a rehearsal. I had no idea who would be there until they came on.

First up was John Tapp, the television racing presenter who had interviewed me a few times over the years. He offered a tribute in his trademark colourful but sincere style, saying the real Spirit of Tasmania was not a boat, but the grit I had shown in fighting back from devastating circumstances.

Mum and Dad were next and although we saw each other every day, we all welled up in tears as if we hadn't seen each other for years. For me, I suppose it was a formal, public acknowledgement of all they had done for me. Having the outside world recognise what we had been through made it a very emotional occasion.

Kim, Naami, and Yvonne Duncan from the Austin joined Mum, Dad, Jason and me on stage and had their say.

The show goes for a lot longer than the half-hour they put to air, but even when the cameras stopped rolling there were more surprises. The audience was made up of friends, racing people and others who had been involved in some way in my recovery. We came straight down off the stage into a cocktail party for the whole crowd.

We ate and drank late into the night and it was great to catch up with people like Jacquie, the physio from the Austin, and Bruce MacDonald, the rider of the horse Theutelle had tripped over. Some of us went back to my hotel and kicked on—and by the end it was not my spinal cord that was making me unsteady on my feet. I had an absolute ball.

I should get out more often, I thought.

'Becky'

16

Men are from Mars and women are from Venus, the human psychologists say. It's the same with horses. Fillies are from Paris, geldings are from Adelaide.

Colts are like teenage boys, rough and boisterous. Cutting them down to size—also known as 'the unkindest cut of all'—fixes that. Gelding a colt turns the wild teenager into a placid young man. He does what he's told, when he's told.

Fillies are generally more sensitive and often need kinder handling. Many need someone to put an arm around them, someone who can make them feel safe. If a filly feels no one cares, that she has no one she can trust, she can turn rebellious.

In a busy stable, it's hard to find the time to attend to the special needs of fillies. They might seem fine but how are they feeling on the inside? A trainer's powers of intuition are as important as techniques of conditioning when it comes to getting the best out of a filly. Just ask Bart Cummings, whose successes in the fillies' classics outnumber his collection of Melbourne Cups, or Neville Begg, who prepared a string of great fillies and mares including Emancipation and the Golden Slipper winner, Dark Eclipse. These men know their fillies like daughters.

For our family there was one special filly. Dad fell in love with her at first sight at the Launceston yearling sales, back in February 1998. We had gone there to bid on a few lots selected for clients. Mum warned Dad specifically not to buy anything on the spur of the moment; our financial position still hadn't recovered fully from the aborted move to Victoria. But Dad was besotted with a bay-coloured filly sired by Weasel Clause, himself a son of the champion sire Marscay. He couldn't believe he got her for only $3000.

On the way home we rang Mum to break the news. 'You said you wouldn't buy anything "on spec",' she said. 'We can't afford it.'

'Wait until you see her,' said Dad. 'She's lovely.'

As soon as we unloaded our small but perfectly formed purchase, Mum agreed we had done the right thing.

That didn't change the fact that we couldn't afford her. We would have to find some partners. I rang Kim and Lenny Dixon and they agreed to take three shares. Mum said we needed to lay off a bit more of the risk to someone else. Given the situation, who else but our bank manager, Stuart Elliss. He came to the party with his son, Brendan, for two shares each. That left Mum and Dad with three shares out of ten. We could handle that.

I gave every horse that came into the stable a nickname. I called this girl 'Becky'. Why? She just seemed like a 'Becky'. Stuart Elliss came up with her official name based on her mother, Etruscan. He looked up a book on the Etruscans, a pre-Christian civilisation based in Tuscany, northern Italy. That led to the name My Sienna, a slight misspelling of the Tuscan town of Siena, where, each July and August, the locals hold the palio, a time-honoured bareback horse race around the 1000-year-old town square.

The first thing we did with our new yearlings was to educate them in the basics of being a racehorse. 'Breaking in', it's called, but that can have connotations of breaking a horse's natural spirit. That's not how Dad did it. He followed the more enlightened modern style, establishing a direct re-lationship with his horses from day one.

The first lesson for a yearling was learning how to respond to directions from the reins. Dad began by putting a head collar on the yearling with two long reins attached. As the horse circled him, he pulled on one rein at a time to intro-duce the young horse to the idea of turning left or right in response to the tug of the leather strap. Once the horse became used to this, he introduced a bit into the mouth, again attached to the long reins, and followed the same process.

The other thing Dad did from day one was establish the idea of having a rider on board. To start with, I would stand beside the yearling and lay my arms on its back for a few minutes. After a few days I added my upper body to the load, still with both my feet on the ground. When the horse accepted that, I did the same thing with my feet off the ground. Step by step we built up trust until I could sit on them bareback. After three or four weeks, if all had gone well, the young student horse accepted a saddle on its back and moved around the stable guided by my movement of the reins.

Most good racehorses are intelligent. Becky certainly had brains, as well as a model's figure. Whatever we taught her one day she could repeat the next. Once our yearlings had learned the basics, we usually sent them out to the paddock to grow for a few months before coming back for a full racing preparation. But we had a hunch there was something special about Becky from the way she had taken to her breaking in. We took her to the track for a couple of gallops before she went to the paddock, a sort of end-of-term test before the holidays.

Her first gallop was up the straight at Spreyton. She had no idea what she was supposed to be doing. She was too busy taking in the new surroundings to concentrate on running flat out, so a couple of days later we took her out with a partner to run alongside and keep her mind on the job. Becky just blew the other horse away. It wasn't just what she did that day that convinced us she was one out-of-the-box. It was the way she did it, her fluent galloping action skimming across the turf with a minimum of effort—a 'daisy cutter', in racing jargon.

I couldn't wait to ride Becky in her first race, but I never got the chance thanks to that ill-fated day at Elwick three months later.

Becky had her first start at Hobart in September 1998—a month after I'd come home from my own 'breaking in' at the Talbot—running an unlucky fifth. She won her next three races in a row. She was something special, all right.

After Christmas Dad set her for the big two-year-old races during the summer carnival. She ran fifth in one and third in the other, but Dad believed that with better luck and better riding she would have been unbeaten.

This wasn't just sour grapes. Dad was prepared to put his money where his mouth was. Eight years after leaving Ballarat with his tail between his legs, this was the horse he would take back to Victoria to show them what he could do, he told the other owners.

There was only one problem. By now Dad had let go of most of his horses so he could concentrate on looking after me. With virtually no training fees coming in, we couldn't really afford to send Dad and Becky to the mainland for a full spring campaign. Besides, Dad didn't want to leave my side.

Stuart Elliss suggested transferring Becky to the Hayes' stable. But when the owners sat down to make a decision, the one thing they all agreed on was that Becky was Dad's little girl and she needed him with her to produce her best. She and Dad just adored each other. In a big stable where nobody knew her little quirks, likes and dislikes, she would not get the attention she needed. If Becky was leaving home for the big city, then Ted was going with her.

Dad planned the campaign with all the detail of a military operation. On a guerrilla budget. Hire a car? No, he'd take the Ford LTD from home. Accommodation? Dad rang around a few contacts from Ballarat. One of the trainers there, Colin Rees, had a property with nice big yards with plenty of grass, which would make Becky feel right at home. Dad could sleep in a spare room in the Reeses' house. Colin's daughter Rhonda could ride Becky in trackwork.

Dad mapped out a race program leading to the ultimate goal of a spring three-year-old filly, the $500 000 Victorian Oaks, held at Flemington two days after the Melbourne Cup. Mum, still smarting from our first Victorian misadventure, was not so keen on paying the early entry fees for the big races.

'You're dreaming,' she told Dad.

'Yes, but what a dream,' he replied.

Dad's diary of 'Operation Becky' records his battle plan down to the hour. Becky left Brigadoon at 5 p.m. on Thursday 5 August 1999, arriving at Ballarat at 1 p.m. the next day. Her first race of the campaign was the William Crockett Stakes at Moonee Valley on 14 August. She drew the outside gate in the 1000-metre dash, so Dad told Greg Hall, who was riding her, to drop back at the start so she would not be caught wide. Greg dropped her so far back she was still last on the turn, and although she passed four rivals in the straight, she crossed the line so far behind the winner—14.5 lengths— she might as well have been in the next race.

Dad's heart sank. Perhaps he really was out of his league in the big smoke. When he rang that night I could hear the disappointment in his voice. I asked him what he planned for Becky next. He said there was a 1400-metre race at Flemington three weeks later, but he wasn't sure if she could step up in distance and win. 'Work her hard,' I said. 'All you have to do is trust yourself and make sure she's fit. She'll do the rest.'

Walking Becky to the track each morning past the house in Kennedy's Road Dad had had to abandon in 1991 gave him an added spur. He'd put too much into this to leave Ballarat empty-handed again.

The Flemington race was make-or-break for 'Operation Becky'. If she didn't run in the placings this time, she would not have enough prizemoney to get a start in the big fillies' races Dad had mapped out leading to the Oaks. When the barrier draw came out, his heart sank again—14 out of 18. To counter that, Dad decided to put on an apprentice, 18-year-old Matthew Gatt, who not only had a 1.5-kilo weight allowance but a good record of recent city success.

Becky was not the only one short of money. Dad's long nightly phone calls to Mum and me had blown his meagre budget. To make up, he saved a strapper's fee by saddling Becky up and leading her around the Flemington mounting yard himself. On a big spring race day, this was virtually unheard of, akin to an AFL coach like Kevin Sheedy polishing the boots of his players before a final.

By the time Becky cantered off to the starting gates Dad was covered in sweat, some of it his own. A glance over to the totalisator board did little for his confidence. My Sienna was the rank outsider at $87.30 for the win and $23.10 for a place.

After the disaster of Moonee Valley, Dad told Matthew to take advantage of the weight allowance and kick up early into a handy position. Matthew followed his instructions to the letter. Coming to the turn, Becky was travelling strongly outside the leader. Behind her the favourites, including the subsequent Caulfield Cup winner Diatribe, were being pushed along. The 450-metre home stretch at Flemington is a long way to hang on to the lead, but Becky fought for every centimetre, winning by a length. Clever girl.

In the grandstand at Flemington, Dad punched the air. The $46 000 for first prize would qualify Becky for all the big races and meant the whole campaign was already paid for.

Back at Brigadoon things had been a little more animated while the race was on. I was up off the sofa screaming my head off all the way down the straight. I had good reason to celebrate—$11 040-worth to be exact. Although I had never been a gambler because of the trouble I had seen it cause many people in the racing game, when you know how good a horse like Becky is and you see her paying close to 100 to 1, you have to have a bet. I put $100 each way on her. I wasn't the only one. So many Tassie punters kept faith with Becky that TABs in Devonport and Launceston ran out of cash that day.

'That's racing.' To people outside our industry, these two words probably translate as 'Bad luck', or the more earthy 'Shit happens'. To jockeys and trainers, whose only daily certainty is uncertainty, it has a much richer meaning.

'That's racing' is the mantra we call upon to blank out the anguish that would otherwise destroy us. You spend months preparing a horse for a big race only for it to get injured, be blocked for a run, or crucified by a bad barrier draw. These are the facts of racing life. If you stopped to let yourself think how unfair it all is—*why does this always happen to me?*—you'd never get out of bed. 'That's racing' is much more than two words to racing people. It's a state of mind. Without it, we'd go out of our minds.

The late Queen Mother understood this. In 1956 her steeplechaser, Devon Loch, was 50 metres from the winning post in the Grand National with no other runner in sight. Either the roar of the crowd, a shadow on the ground or sheer exhaustion made Devon Loch perform a bizarre hop into the air and belly-flop to the ground. By the time the horse and his rider, Dick Francis (later the author of equine thrillers), came to their senses, the next horse into the straight had arrived to score one of the strangest wins in racing history. Dick Francis was at a loss to explain to Her Majesty what had gone wrong. She said it for him: 'That's racing, I suppose.'

My Sienna's next start, in the Tranquil Star Stakes at Caulfield, produced a 'That's racing' moment in the finest Devon Loch tradition.

In a virtual replay of her Flemington run, Becky crossed from a wide gate, kicked clear in the straight and was holding the chasers at bay. With 50 metres to go, Matthew Gatt gave her a crack with the whip. Perhaps she was giving her all and resented the 'persuader'. Perhaps it landed flush on her sensitive hip bone. Whatever the reason, Becky reacted as if she'd had an electric shock. In full flight, she kicked out her back legs, which sent her canoning sideways into the running rail, losing almost all her momentum. By the time she regained her balance, the only runner mounting a serious challenge, Miss Pennymoney, had surged past. There are a lot of ways to get beaten in this game, but you don't see that one very often.

Even the connections of the winner, a blue-blooded filly that cost $200 000, admitted Becky deserved to win. (It was a pity she didn't—I had $500 on her that day, a loss that ended my brief betting career.)

Then things turned really bad. When Becky came out of her stall to go to the track two days later, she had a noticeable limp. When Dad rang that night, all the cheer of his recent calls was gone. The success in Melbourne had done a lot to help Dad's homesickness—this six weeks in Ballarat was the longest he had ever been away from us—but now he was gutted. Just as the curse of the Buckinghams appeared to be breaking—with me back on my feet and 'Operation Becky' beginning to unfold as planned—here was another needle in the doll.

X-rays of Becky's legs showed wear and tear in the tendons around the knee joints, but no bone damage. With ongoing treatment, the vet said, she could take her place in her next targeted race, the $151 000 Edward Manifold Stakes at Flemington. The roller-coaster ride could continue.

This would be the most prestigious race we had ever had a runner in outside the Caulfield Cup. And the gutsy, not to mention spectacular, performance by Becky in the Tranquil Star had made her one of the most widely discussed chances. This time Matthew didn't risk drawing the whip when Becky was challenged in the last 200 metres. Riding hands and heels, he got her home by a long neck. Now she was one of the favourites for the Oaks.

After the Edward Manifold win, a bloodstock agent rang Dad on behalf of a New Zealand stud to offer $400 000 for Becky. It only took a quick discussion with the Elisses, Kim and Lenny to decide to knock it back. The agent upped the offer to $500 000. The answer was still no. This sort of success is what we had lived and worked for all our lives. And besides, Becky would earn much more than that if she won the final three races on our hit list, the One Thousand Guineas, the Wakeful Stakes and the Oaks.

Mum flew over for the Guineas, at Caulfield. She and Dad were invited to the committee room for lunch before the big race. Everything seemed set for another great day.

The favourite was Gai Waterhouse's Danglissa, having her first start in Melbourne after cleaning up the fillies' races in Sydney. Dad knew Danglissa would try to lead all the way, and because the Sydney courses run clockwise—the opposite to Victoria—she was likely to have trouble on the turns. He told Matthew to have Becky up on the pace, but not to get outside Danglissa in case the Sydney filly ran out on the corners.

Everything was going to plan as they raced to the home turn, Danglissa in front, with Becky a length back on the outside. But Matthew made his move slightly too soon. As the pressure went on, Danglissa drifted off the rails, bumping Becky heavily and pushing her wide as they rounded the last bend. All the way down the straight, Danglissa drifted wider on the track, ending up half-way to the outside rail. The Victorian filly Shizu stuck to the inside, saving valuable ground, and thrust her head out on the line to beat Danglissa. Becky fought on valiantly for fourth. Although she would not have won, the buffeting from Danglissa probably cost her a placing.

Since taking the ride at Flemington the first time, Matthew had kept our navy-blue racing silks between races, bringing them to the track himself on Becky's race days. After the Guineas Dad asked him to hand over the colours. Matthew knew what that meant. Dad had been loyal to him, sticking with an apprentice for such a prestigious event when plenty of senior jockeys were available, but in these big races there are no second chances. That's racing.

By the next day word had got around. Jockey managers were ringing Dad trying to get the ride for the Wakeful Stakes on Derby Day, the grand opening of the Melbourne Cup carnival. Damien Oliver could ride her in the Oaks but he already had a booking for the Wakeful. The manager of veteran Greg Hall hounded Dad. Greg Childs, the rider of the champion mare, Sunline, was unavailable. Greg Hall would not take 'no' for an answer. He rang Dad personally and said: 'Ted, I'm telling you I will win the Wakeful for you.' It was an offer too good to refuse.

To the professionals, Derby Day is racing's equivalent of football's Grand Final. The Melbourne Cup still stops the nation, but the rest of the races on the first Tuesday in November are just sideshows to keep the crowd amused before the main event. Derby Day is about quality, proving yourself against the best. The Wakeful runners, most having their first attempt at a middle distance, test each other out five days before the Oaks. The Derby, like an under-21s grand final, is the proving ground where the men of the future separate themselves from the boys.

When you win on Derby Day, you win respect.

With those stakes, Dad was more nervous than usual when he arrived at Flemington for Derby Day 1999. He had been to Derby Day only once before, as a spectator in 1984. That year Red Anchor won the Cox Plate—one of only three three-year-olds to do so in the past 26 years—before taking the Derby the following week. Now that's quality, that's respect.

Dad believed Becky was good enough to turn the tables on Danglissa and Shizu and write her name into Derby Day history. But doubts still stirred in his mind. Had he given her enough strong work to cope with the step up from the 1600 metres of the Guineas to the 2000 metres of the Wakeful? Had he given her too much?

At Brigadoon Mum and I were glued to the television, watching the grand final-sized crowd of more than 87 000 pour into Flemington. As the runners paraded before the Wakeful, my heart rate went up a gear. Becky looked a glowing picture of health, as relaxed amidst the big race buzz as if she were wandering around the paddock at home.

For once she had drawn a good barrier, so she would not have to be used up early to get across to a good position. In the final seconds before the starting gates opened, Greg Hall may have been in the saddle, but mentally I was living this ride as much as he was. *Ease her out of the gates, just let her find her feet. Get her relaxed. Just slot in somewhere midfield.*

Wakeful Stakes, Derby Day 1999

The gates fly open and the camera zooms in on Danglissa. Mouth open and wild-eyed, she fights her rider's pull on the reins as he tries to settle her to a sensible speed. It's a great action shot but where the hell is Becky? The field has gone a few hundred metres before a wide-angle view allows us to pick out Greg Hall in our colours. Becky has found her feet, lobbing along smoothly in midfield. *Good girl.*

Danglissa refuses to settle and tears along in the lead, making the race a true test of stamina. At the halfway mark Becky is about ten lengths behind her, further back than Dad and I planned. *Be patient. Danglissa and those up with her will have to wilt. Make sure Becky has plenty of room so she doesn't get blocked when they fall back through the field.*

Greg is on my wavelength. He's moved Becky up closer to the leading bunch, three or four horses off the rails as heads turn for home. Danglissa is hitting the wall. The filly behind her, Forest Express, takes up the running under hard riding. Inside the last 200 metres the whips are cracking. Three lengths further back, on the edge of the TV screen, Becky is winding up, her front legs flicking out into the smooth rhythm she showed in that first gallop as a yearling. *Let's go girl. Show 'em what you've got!*

Forest Express has the upper hand in her arm wrestle with Danglissa. They lunge towards the finishing post. The roar of the crowd rises to a new pitch as a blur of navy blue swoops down the outside. As the two other fillies throw themselves at the line like Olympic runners stumbling to the tape, Becky steams past at full throttle to win. *You little beauty! Good girl, Becky, good girl.*

At Flemington, Dad and the Ellisses were in that state of shock that descends when your greatest dream, or worst nightmare, arrives in real life. You see it but you don't quite believe it.

Dad had waited twenty years for the chance to prove himself in the big league. In a little over two minutes he had done it. Becky's electrifying finish sucked him up out of his seat in a moment of pure joy. That's all it was, a moment, before deeper feelings seeped to the surface. There was guilt: the daughter who had worked beside him almost every day of those twenty years, the daughter who saw the raw talent in this filly from her first gallop, was not there to share the glory. Doubt: after all our family had been through in the past eighteen months, how long could something this good last? Sorrow: If I had been able to ride Becky, this would have been the breakthrough win my career needed. The win that would earn respect from the people who matter.

The next few minutes were surreal. Bass Strait lay between me on the sofa at Brigadoon and Dad in the winner's enclosure at Flemington, surrounded by cameras and microphones. Yet as Dad spoke through the television, I could feel his pride, his joy and his sorrow. I felt his and I felt mine. Joy and sorrow. Triumph and grief. That's racing.

What a difference a win makes. My Sienna, the Tassie filly the punters wrote off as a no-hoper before her first start at Flemington, was now 2 to 1 favourite for the Oaks. Her trainer, who hardly rated a line in the Melbourne racing press in two years at Ballarat, was the hottest interview in town.

The bloodstock agents were on the phone again. One said My Sienna was one of three fillies he was considering for a client in the United States who was willing to pay up to $1 million. Was Dad interested in selling?

No. He knew that once the Americans saw the x-rays of Becky's damaged knee tissue they would put the cheque book away. Besides, he could not abandon 'Operation Becky' when we were so close to the ultimate conquest, the Oaks.

I had been too self-conscious to go to Melbourne to watch Becky so far, but after a performance like that there was nothing that could keep me away from Oaks Day. On the Thursday night before the Wakeful Stakes, Channel Nine had screened my 'This is Your Life' episode. That did a lot for my confidence about being seen in public again.

I wasn't prepared for the media pack waiting for me at Flemington on Oaks Day. The photographers were ready to pounce when I arrived and I was happy to do the first few interviews. After a while, however, I began to feel claustrophobic as they followed my every shuffle around the course with my walking stick, so I headed down to the horse boxes to be with Becky. That was OK until she had to come out for the big race and the swarm of cameras was back in my face. I could hardly get through them as I made my way to the reserved area where the Victoria Racing Club had provided a place for me to watch the race. On top of the tension of having the favourite in the Oaks, it all became too much. I burst into tears. 'Can you please just give me some room?' I pleaded. As soon as the cameramen realised how upset I was, they lowered their lenses and let me go.

When the barriers opened in the Oaks, I was back in jockey mode. I would have given anything for it to have been me out there on Becky.

Just as in the Wakeful, she quickly settled down towards the back of the field, conserving her energy for the testing 2500-metre journey. Coming to the home turn, Greg Hall began winding her up. Half-way down the straight he put her into overdrive and she cruised up to the lead. Greg seemed confident, looking over his shoulder for any challengers. I was screaming my head off. 'Go Becky! Go Becky!'

This was the vision I had carried in my mind for so long—Becky carrying the navy blue home to win the Oaks. But now there was something wrong with this picture— a filly called Tributes, in the bright pink colours of Australia's biggest owners, the 'Chicken kings' Jack and Bob Ingham. Tributes was lurking behind Becky ready to pounce. Her jockey, Darren Gauci, was saving her for one last surge over the final 100 metres. I'd ridden enough races just as Gauci was doing to see what was about to unfold. Becky's stamina tank was flashing on 'empty'. Tributes still had a little bit up her sleeve.

For a few tormenting seconds everything went into slow motion as the two fillies went to the line. Tributes edged to the front. Becky, now just running on guts and instinct, held on for second place.

The glorious vision wasn't to be, but we'd won one thing: respect.

Bob Ingham invited us into the winning owners' bar. 'I wish you could have won,' he said. His trainer, John Hawkes, was also kind in victory. 'I feel like I've spoilt the party a bit,' he said. 'If my filly had run second I would have been very happy for Bev and her father.'

The track staff had organised a golf buggy to drive me down to Becky's stall after the trophy presentation for the Oaks. Wellwishers in the crowd were calling out from over the fence. 'Great to see you here, Bev', 'Good on you, Bev', 'Good luck, Bev'. That took care of my disappointment at Becky being beaten. It was humbling to think so many people cared so much. I felt wonderful, as if, for a precious few moments, I had snatched back my past life.

Dad and I went to dinner that night—Mum had stayed in Tassie, believing she brought bad luck ever since the Guineas—but we didn't spend much time on post-mortems. We were more interested in the future, on using the day as a launching pad for a second crack at Victoria.

I told Dad how much I liked Benalla, a small town in northern Victoria on the Broken River. He thought it was too far away from the city—200 kilometres up the Hume Highway from Melbourne, but I talked him into at least having a look.

He was impressed by the flat, lush surface of the Benalla racetrack. When the racing club secretary told him local trainers could use it every day he could hardly believe it—at Spreyton you only got a training gallop on the course proper before one of the big races.

By the time Dad got back in the car to drive me back to my hotel, he was sold: when we came back to Victoria, Benalla was a top candidate.

On Monday I flew home. The excitement of Flemington and the hunt for a new home had worn off. I was back in the blues. Disappointment at not riding in the Oaks had turned to bitterness. Distance races had been my forté. If I had ridden

Becky, knowing her so well, surely it would have made the difference between losing and winning. When Dad and I had had success in the past, it had always been the two of us, 'The Team'. This time I wasn't in the game. I didn't feel part of the team. I felt cheated of all the things I wanted most.

After a well-deserved rest at home, Becky returned to Melbourne in February for her autumn campaign. After a couple of runs her troublesome knees gave out. She had to have an operation to repair the damaged cartilege and remove bone chips.

The operation appeared to be a success, so Dad planned another Victorian raid for the 2000 spring carnival. At her first start, at Flemington, it was obvious her knees were not right. Dad retired her on the spot.

It was a big blow to him. Dad and Becky had become very close through spending so much time together on the road. Becky got to know the sound of Dad's LTD so well that every time he drove past her paddock at Ballarat she would run to the fence and whinny to him. He'd pull over, rub her nose and tell her how beautiful she was. If it was late at night and Dad needed to go out, he would have to borrow the Reeses car so he wouldn't disturb her.

Although Becky's racing days came to an end before she fulfilled her potential, Dad thought he had plenty to look forward to from her foals. Not all the owners agreed. Some were not interested in breeding from her, and those who were had different opinions on which stallion she should go to. In the end there was no consensus, so the only solution was to sell her.

The day the float arrived at Brigadoon to take her away was another tough one for Dad. His little girl was leaving home again, this time for good. Becky trotted up to the gate, thinking Dad had just come to rub her muzzle and whisper her name. If she was as smart as I think she was, she would have sensed something was up from the quiver in his voice.

Becky was sold for $260 000 at the Sydney broodmare sales, to Gerry Harvey, the Harvey Norman billionaire. It's comforting to know she's living out her broodmare days in the plush surrounds of his Baramul stud farm in the Hunter Valley. Our share of the sale proceeds came in handy, too. Dad would happily have given it all back, though, to watch Becky grow old in the front paddock, and to hear the patter of little hooves from her children. But that's racing.

Jason

17

Becky's stellar performances in the spring of 1999 brought a fresh mood of hope to Brigadoon. From the middle of the year, I had started to go downhill again.

After I'd got back on my feet I thought I would just keep improving steadily to the point where I'd be almost as fit, strong and mobile as I'd been before. I wasn't going to accept anything less. As the weeks went by, after Naami said she'd done all she could for me, I reached a plateau in my recovery. It began to sink in that this would be as good as I would get, limping along as if I had wooden legs, exhausted after a couple of hours of being up and about, always only a step away from an ungainly tumble.

When I looked out the window, all I could see were the beautiful horses I would never ride again. When Dad drove off to the races with one of them in the float, it was another reminder that 'The Team' had played its last game. I sank into a deep depression and went onto anti-depressant medication. Before my hands had recovered their flexibility, I couldn't even turn the pages of a book—I filled my spare hours watching daytime TV. I still find it hard to believe I became addicted to 'Days of our Lives'.

The success of 'Operation Becky', and the hope that she brought, helped snap me out of my slump.

After the Oaks in November, Jason and I decided to take the trip to Dubai that came with the Racing Media Association 'Personality of the Year' award I had won in March.

It should have been a second honeymoon but it didn't turn out that way. Over the previous few months Jason had been going out more and more on his own. He'd always enjoyed socialising, and before my fall I was always ready for a party once the stable duties were done. But even after I got rid of my crutches I felt self-conscious about my appearance. My weight had ballooned up to 68 kilos, about 30 per cent over my riding weight, and I felt extremely unattractive.

I was willing to go and visit close friends, but I couldn't enjoy myself if I was out in public. If Jason suggested going out I would say no, I'd rather not, but I felt it was unfair to deny him having a social life. He would go out fishing on the river, to footy training, parties, or his parents' place. With few horses in work, there was little for him to do around the stables and he was always complaining of being bored.

'I'm here with you all day, so why can't I go out at night?' he'd say.

In Dubai we went out on sightseeing tours during the day, had dinner in the hotel restaurant in the evening and then I would be ready for bed. The hot climate helped my mobility, but it was still hard work getting around and I was tired by the end of the day. Jason wanted to hit the nightclubs. I'd go up to the room and leave him with the barman.

Since we had been married, Jason and I had talked quite often about having children. He had been keen to start a family before my accident. When I was first in intensive care and the doctors explained the extent of my injuries, one of the first questions he asked was whether I would still be able to have children. The doctors assured him my reproductive system was intact.

I had never had much to do with babies. Being an only child, there were no nieces or nephews in the family. And whenever I was shown a newborn by acquaintances who had become proud parents, I didn't melt into maternal cluckiness. About the only time I had held an infant was when I was still riding. Another jockey, Dale Hicks, brought his wife and baby to the races at Mowbray one day. I was standing closest to him when he announced he had to hop on the scales and thrust his little bundle of joy into my arms. I didn't know what to do. I cradled the child stiffly out in front of me as if I was holding a bomb about to go off and couldn't give Dale his baby back quick enough.

As time went on I came to feel I would like to have children, but not until I retired from riding. When I recovered my mobility after the fall, and it was clear I would never ride professionally again, I went to see my doctor, who assured me there was nothing to prevent me from conceiving and carrying a baby. The only consequence from my injuries would be having to have a Caesarian delivery as my stomach muscles weren't strong enough to push a baby out. That suited me fine—I'd heard enough horror stories from slight-framed lady jockeys who had agonised through 24-hour labours.

In early 2000 the future seemed a little brighter, with Becky preparing for another raid on the rich races in Melbourne, and Dad and I scouring the Internet for potential training bases in Victoria.

Jason had flown over to Melbourne to be Becky's strapper for her big wins in the spring, and he and Dad had spoken about Jason one day becoming a trainer. Perhaps he and I could be training partners.

In January, Jason and I talked about starting our own family and we both felt the time was right. Despite the doctor's assurances, I was a bit apprehensive about how my body would cope with a pregnancy, and the responsibility of being a parent was also quite scary, especially for someone who hadn't had much experience with little children.

I knew I had fallen pregnant before any of the classic indicators. I had always been in tune with my body and at the end of March I sensed what had happened. I bought a home pregnancy test kit and felt a tingle of nervous pleasure when it confirmed what my body had told me. I broke the good news to Jason and he was over the moon. He rang his parents straight away and they were very excited, already talking about shopping for baby clothes. Mum and Dad were thrilled, too. The gods, at last, were smiling on us again.

Not for long, though.

The following week, Jason went off to pre-season footy training one night in my Celica. He usually had a couple of beers at the footy club, dropped one of his mates off and was home for dinner around 8 p.m.

When he hadn't shown up by 8.30 this night I started to get worried. By 9 p.m. I was anxious enough to get in his Falcon and drive up the main road for a few kilometres.

When it dawned on me that I didn't know who he was dropping off that night or where they lived, I turned around and headed home. Besides, Jason knew these roads like the back of his hand, I told myself. Then again, like me, he was inclined to be lead-footed.

As I coasted into the garage, I noticed a police car pull in behind me. Given my record behind the wheel—I'd lost my licence a couple of times for speeding—my first thought was, 'What have I done wrong?'

'Was I speeding?' I asked the officer.

'No, I'm afraid I've got some bad news,' he said. 'It's your husband.'

'What's he done?'

'He's had an accident. He's been taken to hospital.'

'I'll kill him,' I said, thinking he'd broken a leg or something like that. 'How bad is it?'

'He's in a coma. Would you like a lift to the hospital?'

Even then I don't think the full impact of those terrible words sank in, because I calmly told the officer no, that would not be necessary and thank you, but I had better go inside and tell my parents.

Jason

As I walked to the house I felt a tight knot forming in the pit of my stomach, worse than any morning sickness. My heart began to pound in panic.

Mum rang Jason's mother, Judy, and we met her, his father, Mickey, and his sister in the waiting room of the emergency department at Mersey Hospital. We couldn't get anybody to tell us exactly what had happened or how badly injured Jason was. There was talk of Jason having brain damage and spinal damage—the only definite thing was that he was in a coma.

I wasn't allowed in to see him until after midnight. I saw straight away that he had involuntary movement in his arms and legs so, thank God, he hadn't badly damaged his spinal cord.

Then a doctor explained the severity of Jason's head injuries. He had lost control going around a corner on River Road. The car hit a tree, which was probably what stopped it going into the Mersey River. The right side of Jason's head had smashed into the door frame. He had internal bleeding on the brain and if it continued they would have to operate or he could die. He would have to be transferred to the Royal Hobart immediately, where Dr John Liddell's neurosurgery team was on standby.

Although Jason and I had been together for six years, I was still not close to his family. We got on fine on a superficial level but that was largely just politeness. For the previous couple of years Jason had gone to visit his family alone on Christmas Day—I excused myself because of my health problems. The stress of his accident soon exposed the shallowness of my relationship with my in-laws.

I was up all night after Jason's accident. Kim Dixon drove me to Hobart, arriving about 3.30 in the morning. At 5 a.m. a nurse came out to the waiting room and whispered a quick message: 'I'm not supposed to tell you this but they've done some brain scans and it's looking pretty good.'

Twenty minutes later the doctors came out and confirmed the good news. Although Jason would be in a coma for some time, he did not appear to have suffered severe, permanent brain damage.

With that, I felt assured enough to leave the hospital. I had organised rooms for Jason's family and Kim and me at a motel about fifteen minutes away that was run by a racehorse owner I used to ride for.

Later that morning Kim and I went back to see Jason in the intensive care unit. By then Jason's brother had arrived from Queensland. He made a comment about only immediate family members being allowed on the ward and that Kim was not family. That made my blood boil but I let it pass.

Another bone of contention with my in-laws was the media conference I appeared at the day after Jason was admitted to the Royal Hobart. The hospital had been besieged with calls from reporters, and I asked the hospital to organise one session to deal with them all at once. I didn't think Jason's family would want the added stress and I felt I could handle it because I'd been through it all before. I thought I was doing them a favour by not troubling them with it.

Jason's family were upset at not being invited, and I felt real hostility between us. I began going in to see Jason outside visiting hours to avoid us all sitting around the bed in awkward silence.

It was hard to believe I was back in the same intensive care ward where I had been a patient barely two years before, only now it was my husband being fed through a tube in his nose, unable to speak or go to the toilet for himself. I'd sit there for hours, just watching the rise and fall of his breath.

Given the trouble I was having with morning sickness, it suited me to come in about nine in the morning, before Jason's family arrived—this enabled us to keep out of each other's way, and ensured Jason always had someone with him.

It turned out that Jason did need an operation to drain fluid off his brain. Dr Liddell and his surgeons drilled two holes in the back of his skull, taking the pressure off his brain in much the same way as removing the burst disc had relieved my spinal cord.

And as with my injury, there was no clear picture from the doctors of exactly how much permanent damage had been done. They couldn't tell us when Jason would come out of his coma, let alone what he would be like when he did come to.

During the long hours sitting next to his helpless, hibernating body, I wondered how we would cope with the needs of a newborn child, with me not fully independent and Jason perhaps permanently immobilised. And what if, with our luck, the baby had serious medical problems? I decided to have an amniocentesis test: if my baby had a serious abnormality, such as Down's syndrome, I needed to know now. Fortunately the results showed everything was progressing normally. Even better, it revealed I would be having a girl, exactly what I wanted.

It was a shame, though, that this exciting news was lost on Jason when he first flickered his eyes open more than a week after the crash. I could see he was unable to focus, and nothing I said registered. He didn't recognise Dad or some of his own best friends when they came in to visit.

Day after day, for four weeks, we waited for a sign that Jason was back with us. Gradually his periods of consciousness became longer, and his facial expressions indicated he knew who I was—but he couldn't speak to let me know for sure. I kept faith though, because my own experience told me that although the human body might look crushed beyond repair, it had an amazing capacity to recover from trauma, especially if it was young and fit beforehand.

And so it was with Jason. After a month he began to understand what was being said to him, although his short-term memory was non-existent; the moment he heard something he had forgotten it. He also started to be able to express himself. His first word was 'more', pointing to his ice cream bowl. He would point at the television set and say 'TV' when he wanted it switched on. His eyes followed the action on the screen but if he was watching a football game he could not tell you who had been playing less than a minute after the final siren.

In May, Jason's doctors decided he was in good enough shape to move closer to home, to Launceston, to begin his rehabilitation program. He had suffered no permanent brain damage, but after so long in a coma he would have to learn as a grown-up the most basic things even a child can do—walk, talk, catch a ball—all over again.

Jason had a room of his own on the sixth floor of Launceston Hospital. Although he was confined to a wheelchair when not in bed, he had learned to use the telephone and some short-term memory was coming back—he could remember part of the ambulance ride from Hobart to Launceston.

I would drive down every day from Brigadoon to visit him and take him around the grounds in his wheelchair for a bit of a break from the sterile corridors of the wards. He had been there for me in my hour of need and now I could repay him.

I also checked out his rehabilitation sessions at the gym. Right from the start I could see he was in the same situation I had been in at the Talbot—too many patients for the staff to be able to focus on his needs for the whole session. Even before he started exercising, Jason had been complaining of a sore right shoulder. I'd mentioned it a couple of times to nurses and doctors but there was no follow-up. Each day a doctor would pay a quick visit in the morning, but Jason still wasn't up to explaining the nature of his shoulder soreness. If there were no problems in the written nurses' reports, the doctor would be gone quicker than you could say 'more public health funding'. Officially, there was no problem with his shoulder.

Jason's accident had affected the parts of his brain that coordinated his body's movement. The physiotherapists started by having him on his hands and knees so that he would not fall over as they worked on re-establishing his brain–limb interaction. The sore shoulder restricted his movement and distracted his concentration so he wasn't getting the full benefit of the treatment. On top of this he was having trouble hearing because of damage to his right ear, which had also not yet been properly diagnosed.

When the rehab staff moved Jason on to standing, supporting himself by holding onto parallel bars, I could see his shoulder pain stopping him in his tracks. That was when I first started thinking about taking him out of hospital and organising our own program at home.

Before Jason's accident, Mum and Dad had booked a holiday to England. They offered to cancel it to help out but I told them they should go; Kim would come over if I needed any help.

Shortly after Mum and Dad flew out, Jason was allowed home for a weekend. The hospital staff were a bit reluctant to let him go, and started to explain that there were a lot of dangers for a person in a wheelchair in a house that had not been especially adapted for disabled access.

'Don't worry, our house is wheelchair-friendly,' I said.

I had my old wheelchair ready for Jason when he got out of the car at Brigadoon, and Kim and I used my slideboard to transfer him in and out of bed—he didn't have the strength to shift himself because of his shoulder.

Jason loved being at home. His spirits picked up noticeably over the weekend and he became quite upset on the Monday morning when we packed him into the car to go back to hospital.

I wanted to talk to his physio after he had been checked in. I was told someone would be around within the hour. More than two hours later, I was still sitting next to his bed waiting to get someone to discuss his shoulder problem with me. This was the last straw.

'Do I have to keep Jason here?' I asked one of the nurses.

'It didn't come from me, but you can check him out whenever you like,' he said.

'Right,' I thought to myself. 'I'm going to ring Naami and see if she will treat Jason at home. We've done this once, we can do it again.'

Naami agreed to come over five or six days a week, and the hospital recommended an occupational therapist and speech therapist. They met as a team to work out a plan for Jason. I waited until Naami was signed up before telling Jason's mother about my plan because I knew she would be concerned about me taking him out of the doctors' care. I wanted to be able to show her he would be having the best specialist treatment possible at our place.

When I rang to tell her the good news—Jason was back at Brigadoon under the supervision of the physiotherapist who got me back on my feet—she made it clear she wasn't happy. Ten minutes later the phone rang. It was Jason's father. He was angry as well, asking what right I had to override the hospital. I pointed out that Jason was due to come home in about a week's time anyway, but that didn't seem to make any difference. A few minutes later Jason's sister was on the phone wanting to know what I thought I was up to. By the time I put the phone down I was in tears. I'd expected them to be as thrilled as I was to have Jason back at home but now I was wondering whether I'd made a terrible mistake.

Sitting there all alone, in my second trimester of pregnancy and with my husband totally dependent on me, I felt overwhelmed. When Mum rang late that night from England I was almost hysterical. Mum was so alarmed at the state I was in she decided to cut short the holiday and fly home immediately.

Before my parents could get home, I had another fight with Jason's family. If he was going to be out of hospital, then they wanted him to come to their house for a family homecoming. When I explained that the doctors had told me it was important to keep him at Brigadoon for the first month out of hospital so he was in a stable, familiar environment with as little emotional stress as possible, they hit the roof.

The bad blood continued for the next month until Jason recovered enough to travel to his parents' house. His mother would drive to our place to see him for an hour on Saturdays, but his father only came once. For Jason's sake, I exchanged pleasantries with his mother but I'm sure he picked up on the tension.

It was comforting that Naami and her team assured me I had done the right thing. Naami went straight to work on Jason's shoulder, working on the ligaments and tendons that had frozen its movement.

The speech therapist gave Jason lists of words to practise. His pronunciation was slurred, so the idea was for him to read groups of words that sounded alike until a listener could distinguish each one from the others.

The occupational therapist gave him writing drills and left balls of plasticine for him to squeeze when she was gone to build up the dexterity in his hands.

They all agreed Jason had enough strength, it was just a matter of getting his movements coordinated again. Naami put him to work on the standing frame in my makeshift bedroom rehab centre and within ten days he was ready to try his first solo walk. He stood behind the wheelchair, leaning over with his hands on the arm rests. Naami was right behind him, ready to catch him if he faltered. As if in slow motion, with his eyes fixed in concentration, he edged the wheelchair forward across the room, retracing my own first, shuffling steps. Jason may not have been able to speak properly but his beaming smile said it all.

As he progressed Naami made the tasks more complex. When he was able to walk with good balance, she got him to reach out and touch his nose as he went, or look up at the sky. This might sound simple, but when you have lost your sense of balance, it is maddeningly difficult. It took weeks before Jason could go through Naami's routines without a stumble, and as he progressed I had to push him harder and harder to put in the effort required to take him to the next level. I couldn't understand why he was content to just wait for improvement—when I'd been like that, I went at it as hard I could, determined to make it to a new level every day.

When Jason was having trouble with his confidence, at least I could tell him, without fear of contradiction, that I knew how he felt. One night he replied, his eyes welling with tears, with eight words that said a lot more than he intended: 'Now I know what you were going through.' These simple words brought home to me how much intimacy we had lost in the months leading up to Jason's accident.

From the day we met, Jason had been very affectionate. He was always telling me how much he loved me and he was a big-time cuddler, even after we were married. In the months leading up to his accident we had lost that.

In the past, we'd also been as quick to argue—over the small things that most couples do—as cuddle. I realised I had been blocking out the fact that we no longer did much of either, just as I'd shut myself off from the bills piling up at Ballarat, and gone into denial after my fall.

Early in Jason's rehabilitation at home he told Mum, 'Somebody's given me a good kick in the pants to make me realise what Bev's been through.'

But once Jason was walking and looking after himself independently at the end of his ten-week rehab program, it didn't take him long to forget that.

He withdrew into himself and stopped being so affectionate. It was as if when his memory was wiped out he went back to being the Jason I first went out with, the one who bought me roses and told me I was the most beautiful woman he'd ever seen. As things came back to him and he became more aware of how life was now, he became more remote.

He started to complain again about being bored and often went into town for the day. He'd ask me to come along, but being heavily pregnant made me tired and I had to spend long periods resting in bed. It was not just the burden of the baby—my recovery had stopped well short of being able to walk around town for hours. Sometimes, as he walked out the door, I'd ask if he would stay and keep me company.

'Why?' he would ask.

The obvious answer was, 'Because I'm your wife, I'm going to have your baby, and I want you to make me feel safe, loved and secure. I want to know that you still feel like cuddling up to me just as much when I'm overweight, exhausted and nauseous as when I was slim, fit and famous.'

Looking back, I was probably thinking along these lines subconsciously but I certainly never said those things. I couldn't have coped with what might have resulted from confronting Jason. With all my other emotional baggage, there was no room to contemplate losing the father of my child on top of losing my career and physical wellbeing.

Mum had seen the danger signs, though, and recognised them. So much so that by September, five months after Jason's crash, when he was invited to a jockey's stag night, Mum asked Dad to go along to keep an eye on things.

I dropped Jason and Ted off at a Chinese restaurant in town. From there, I would learn later, they kicked on to a pub. A woman who joined their party flirted with Jason. By the end of the night they were kissing.

Dad stepped in and pulled Jason aside. 'That's no way for a married man to carry on,' he told Jason. 'I'm leaving.'

Jason caught up to him outside, and Dad said he wouldn't tell me about it this time but it had better not happen again.

The next day Jason and I went to the jockey's wedding. I didn't feel up to following on to the reception, but I told

Jason I didn't mind him going. The girl from the pub was at the reception.

During the following week, Jason took a lot of messages on his mobile phone. He'd go outside to make the return call, which was unusual. A few times he went into the bathroom after the phone beeped. I asked him why he felt he had to leave the room to answer the phone.

'Just checking my messages,' he said.

I let it go at that.

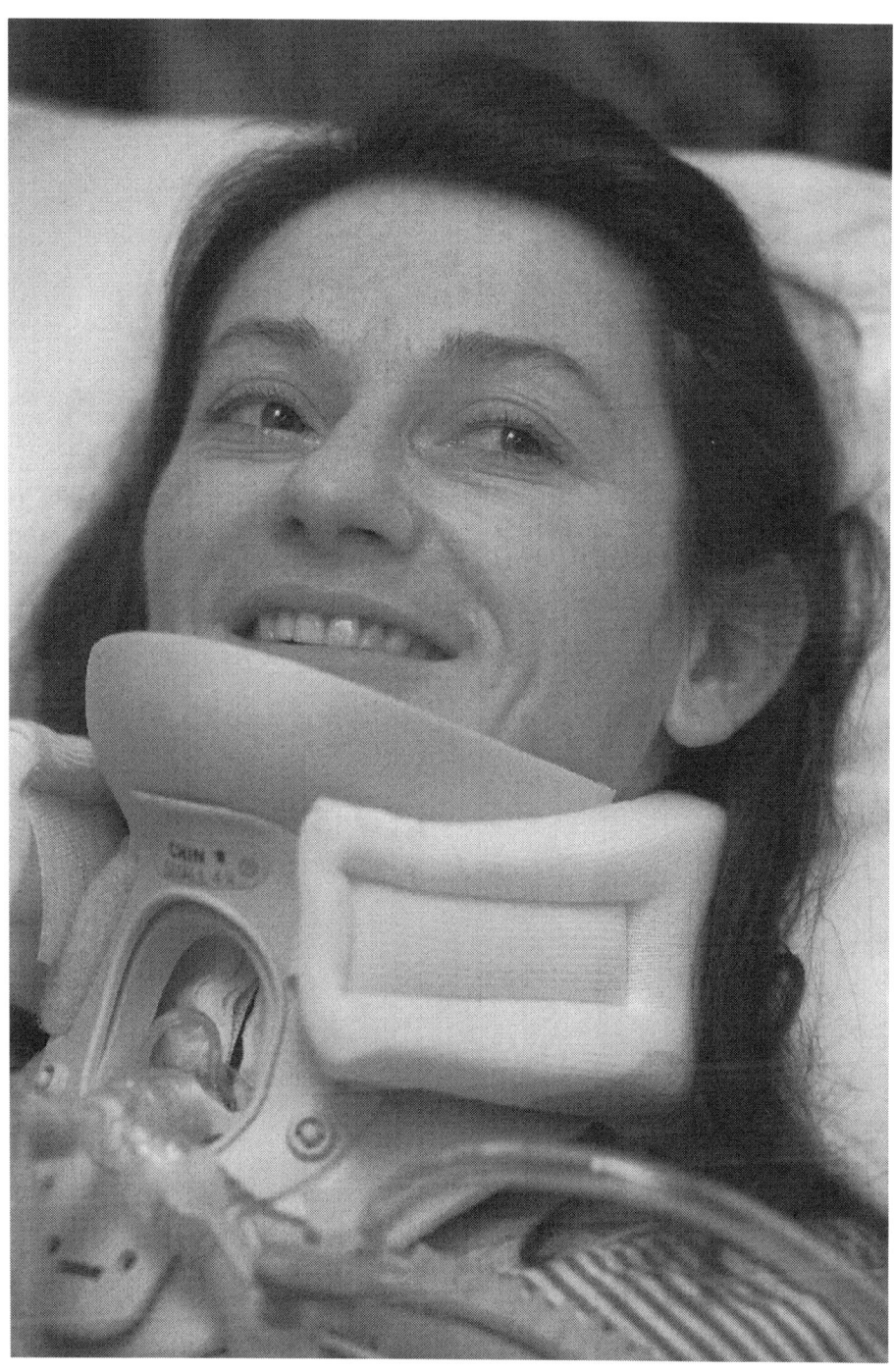

Brave face. In the early days at the Austin Hospital it hadn't sunk in that my career as a jockey was suddenly over. (Courtesy Herald and Weekly Times Photographic Collection)

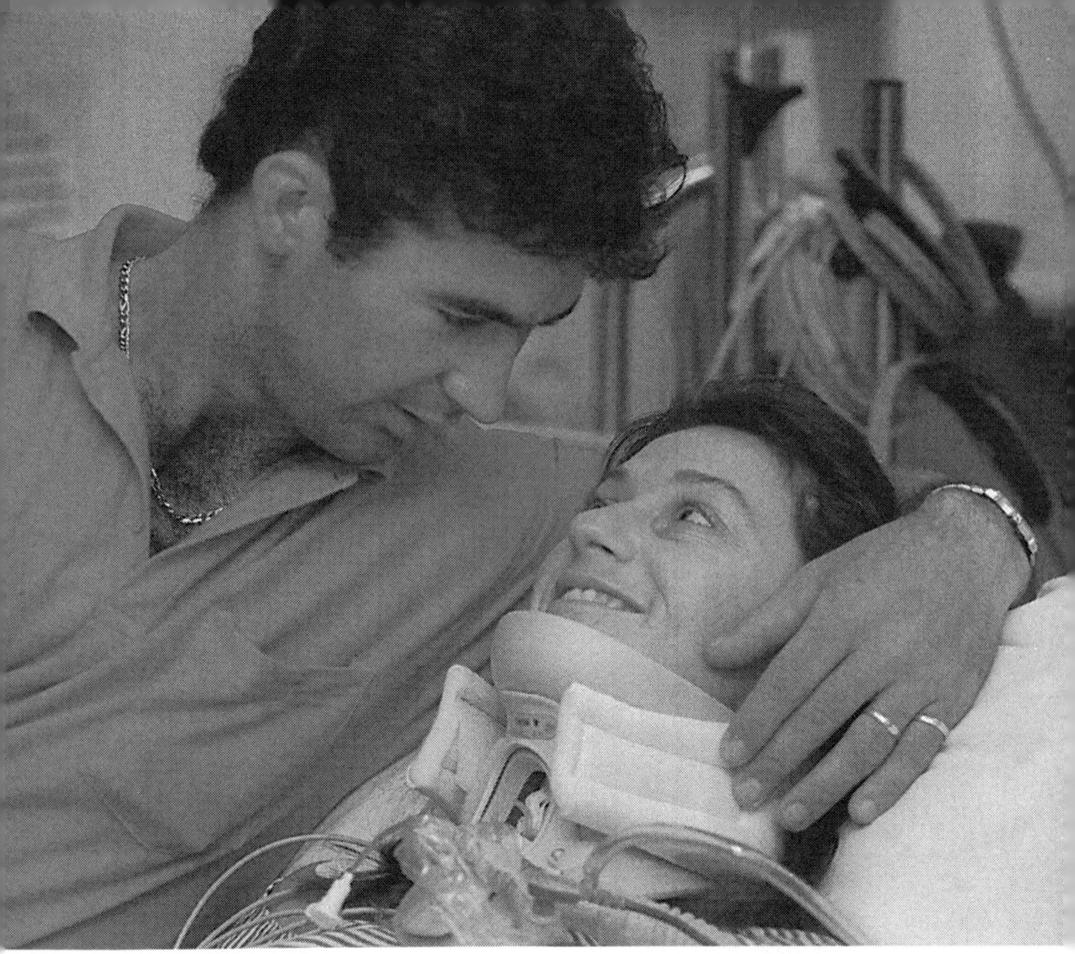

Above: **Love is in the air.** Of all the family, Jason appeared to cope with the trauma of my accident the best. (Courtesy Herald and Weekly Times Photographic Collection)

Right: **Trouble spot.** The burst disc in my neck that crushed my spinal cord had to be cut out by surgeons and replaced by a bone graft.

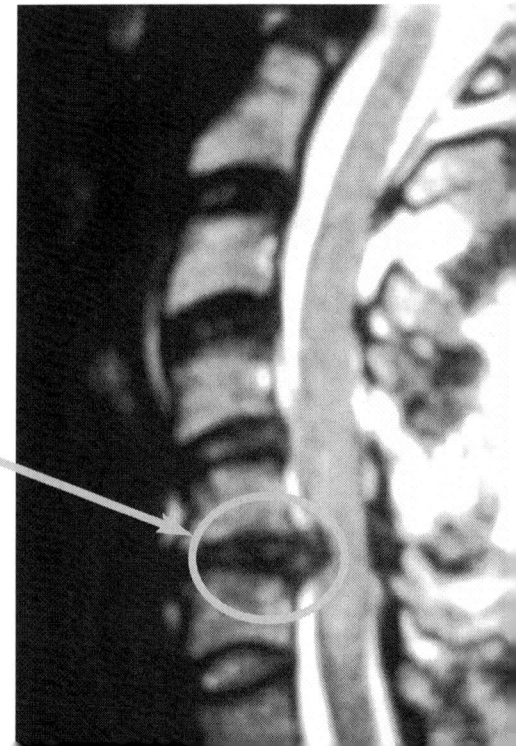

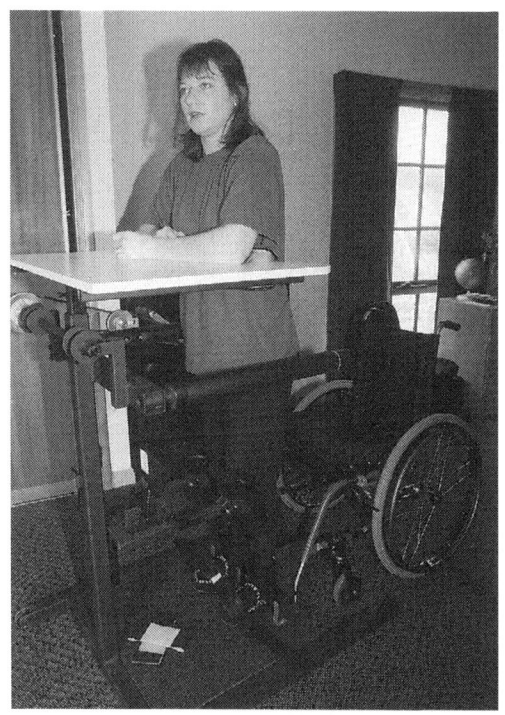

Road to recovery. Using the standing frame in my home rehab unit, I built up my power to stand. (Courtesy *The Mercury*)

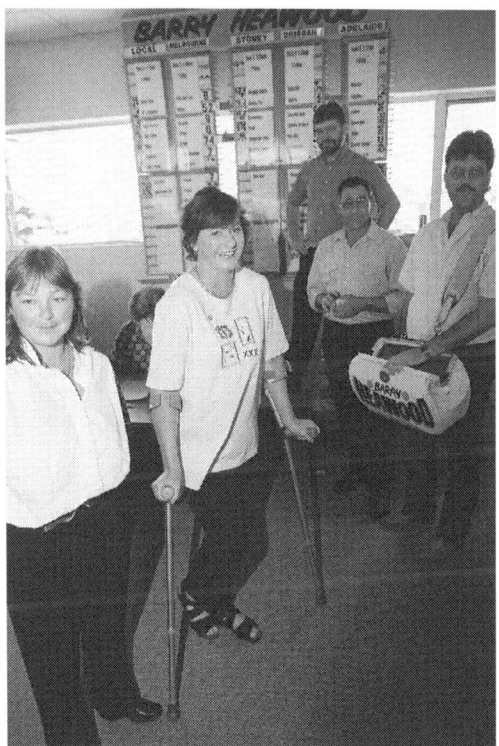

Back on my feet. Returning to the races with Kim Dixon in January 1999.
(Courtesy *The Mercury*)

Getting back on the horse. Dolly, my part-Clydesdale mount, on our property at Benalla, with my darling daughter, Tara, and Mum and Dad.

'I'm leaving you'

18

Jason continued to have trouble hearing in his right ear, which turned out to be caused by a dislodged bone in his eardrum. He was booked in to have day surgery at Launceston Hospital on 26 September. It was about a week after the stag night incident. The same day Dad was catching the ferry with Becky to Melbourne for her 2000 spring campaign, which would end before she had the chance to repeat her deeds of the year before.

We got up early and I drove Jason to Launceston. The operation was due at 11 a.m. so an hour before, a nurse gave Jason a tablet to help him relax before he had his anaesthetic. He was sitting on a bed in a private room and we were just chatting about the surgical procedure when he said: 'I've got something to tell you after the operation.'

'Tell me now,' I said, thinking he'd probably forget by then.

'I'm leaving you. I've met someone else.'

I couldn't believe my ears.

'Don't stir me up, Jason,' I said. 'Why are you teasing me like that?'

'I'm not teasing. I'm leaving you. I've met someone else.'

'You have not, you're lying . . . When could you have met someone else?'

'At the buck's night. Look, here's her phone number,' he said, showing me the display on his mobile phone.

'What's her name?'

He told me. 'I'm in love with her.'

I got up out of my chair, grabbed the phone and slapped him across the face. His expression of disbelief would have given mine a run for its money.

Then someone came to wheel Jason away to the operating theatre.

I wandered through the hospital corridors in a complete daze. I found my way out to the car and slumped over the steering wheel.

When I managed to gather myself together I rang Mum.

'He's left me,' I sobbed.

Mum was shocked and tried to settle me down so that I was in a fit state to drive home.

I rang Kim, who also tried to console me but it wasn't having much effect.

I still had Jason's phone. I found the number Jason had shown me and rang it.

'This is Bev Buckingham. What are you doing trying to break up my marriage?'

The woman made no attempt to hide what was going on—in fact, she made no apology for her interest in Jason.

It was stiff bickies for me, she said—although those weren't the words she used and her tone was very aggressive.

'I'm seven months pregnant and you're breaking up my marriage . . . ' I screamed back before the line went dead.

By chance my friend Dianne Parish turned up. She was flying out that day to Sydney to watch the last few days of the Olympic Games and, with a bit of time to kill in Launceston before her flight, she had dropped in to wish us luck for Jason's surgery.

She arrived while Jason was recovering from the operation and she couldn't work out why I wasn't in the waiting room.

'Where's Bev?' she asked Jason, when she was allowed in to see him.

'I don't know. I've just told her I'm leaving her,' he replied. 'I've found someone else.'

'You're joking,' said Di.

'No, I'm not.'

Di found me in the carpark, still in a mess.

She took me back inside for a cup of coffee and comforted me until she had to leave to catch her plane.

Then I went up to see Jason. I didn't know what to expect. He was still detached, not showing any real emotion.

'I don't expect you to take me home,' he said.

'It's all right, I'll take you home.'

He packed up his things quietly and we walked out to the car.

It didn't take long before I was in tears. I asked him what had brought all this on but he didn't want to talk about it.

'I'll leave tomorrow if you like,' was all he offered.

'You'll leave tonight,' I shot back.

He seemed surprised at the anger in my voice and for the rest of the trip he just stared out the window.

When we pulled into the driveway at Brigadoon, Dad was leaving with Becky on the float and didn't have time to talk. He went over to Jason, they exchanged a few words and shook hands, then Dad left.

Jason rang a friend who lived not far from his new flame, and packed a few things in a bag. His friend arrived a short time later to pick him up and, after six and a half years together, that was how it ended—more with a whimper than a bang.

I rang Jason's mother and told her what had happened.

'Where is he now?' she asked.

Her main concern seemed to be that Jason had gone to a friend's rather than home after leaving Brigadoon, although she did offer me some sympathetic words.

Dad rang Jason from Victoria the next day to try to talk him into coming back. Jason told him he'd think about it, so Dad rang Mum and told her and me to go around and see him.

When we got there Jason's friend's wife was giving him hell over leaving me two months before our child was due. It didn't seem to be having a lot of impact.

I said, 'We're having a baby, surely you can wait to see how things go. Stay for her sake.'

'You shouldn't do that just for the sake of a child,' he said.

'I'll do whatever you want if you come back,' I pleaded.

He said he would consider it if I promised we would move to our own house, closer to his mother and father. This was something he had suggested before, when I was recuperating, but not with the condition that if I didn't agree that would be the end of our marriage. At that time I had felt I needed the support of Mum and Dad—besides, the practicalities of getting another house modified to my disability needs had made it seem virtually impossible.

But now I said OK, we could get our own place when the baby was born. Jason replied that it was too late for that. Even so, when I left that night I still thought there was some hope of a reconciliation.

Within a couple of days, Jason's friend's wife told him she didn't want him staying at her house any more, so Jason went back to live at home.

Over the next couple of weeks it became apparent he was not serious about trying to rescue our relationship. I would go over and pick him up and we would go for a drive and talk around in circles. Nothing would convince him to come back to Brigadoon. He talked about going to live in Queensland, near his brother, and about getting a new job. 'Racing's not the be-all and end-all,' he said.

By then Dad had told me about what had gone on at the stag night. As I dropped Jason off at the end of one of these fruitless sessions I said, 'By the way, I know you've slept with her.'

'How did you know?' he blurted out.

'I didn't, but you've just told me.'

About a fortnight after he left, he told me he had stopped seeing his new love and I thought there was still a glimmer of hope for us, but then I found out he wasn't telling the truth. For me, that was the last straw. Now it sunk in that the man I was supposed to spend the rest of my life with didn't want me any more, and that I was going to be bringing a baby into the world on my own. I sank into a depression worse than anything that followed my fall.

At least with my fall I could blame fate—I had no control over what happened that day at Elwick. This was much more personal. I couldn't fathom how Jason could turn his back on me—he'd told me he loved me. I must have done something to drive him away.

I cried myself to sleep at night, racking my brain for what I'd done to deserve being abandoned. That in turn developed into a consuming fear that the stress and anxiety I was feeling might affect my little girl. How could something so delicate, now such an integral part of me, not be picking up on the grief that had taken hold of me?

I've spent a lot of sleepless nights trying to work out what changed between the beginning of 2000, when Jason wanted to start a family with me, and September, when he declared that he wouldn't try to save our marriage just for the sake of our child.

I don't think it was the girl at the buck's night. Within a few weeks of leaving me, that affair was over.

The obvious explanation would be the car crash—that his brain damage somehow changed his personality. I don't buy that either. By September, Jason wasn't 100 per cent physically and mentally where he was before the crash, but he was the same Jason, just with a foggier memory and not in any shape to be playing footy.

The only thing I can sheet home to his accident is that it may have reminded Jason he would only get one life. He was still only 27, and perhaps coming so close to losing his future at that age made him think there were better ways of spending it than looking after a recovering cripple and raising a daughter. In one of our chats in the weeks after he left, he told me he wanted to live life and have fun while he was still young, have his own place and be his own boss.

It's also fair to say that the woman he left was not the woman he married. On my wedding day I didn't know the meaning of the word 'can't'. 'Women ride against men, we can't have that,' they used to say. Well, I'd helped throw that patronising piece of discrimination in the dustbin. 'OK, we'll let women ride, but we all know they can't beat the best of our brave, tough Tassie men.' Ditto.

When I was a top-line jockey I worked hard, played hard and had the confidence to take on anything, or anyone. The fall changed all that. When it finally sank in that I could never ride in a race again—that I would never walk normally again—I started to dwell on all the things I couldn't do. I lost the confidence to go out and mix with people. I put on weight. Instead of being an outgoing, successful and dynamic partner who made things happen in our marriage, I had become withdrawn, gloomy and passive. 'Can't' became part of my vocabulary for the first time.

Still, when I said my wedding vows—especially that bit about 'for richer and poorer, in sickness and in health'— I meant it with all my heart. I trusted that Jason did as well.

After he left, he brought up things like having our own house and there being more to life than racing as being his reasons for leaving me, but to me these looked like weak excuses. When I'd said I'd agree to us moving away from Mum and Dad after the baby was born, he had said it was too late. And racing's still a big part of his life. Since we've split, the only jobs Jason has had are in racing stables.

My accident changed our lives so quickly and drastically that I don't think Jason was ready for it. He didn't have the inner drive to take up the running when I lost my career and confidence. When we first started going out I asked him: 'If you could have any car in the world, what would it be?' 'A Toyota Hilux,' he said. Me, I wanted a Ferrari. My dream was to have my own private jet and fly to Paris for breakfast. Jason was quite content to spend his life driving a Hilux around suburban Latrobe, having his mates over for a few beers on the weekend.

That difference in our ambitions and life experience didn't seem to matter when I was swept up in chasing premierships and we were on the social A List. When all that vanished it left a vacuum Jason couldn't fill, either for himself or for me.

Yet for months after Jason left, in my heart, I still loved him. I suppose I was still in the denial phase. I had seen his affectionate side and I knew he could be a good father.

Now I have no love left for Jason. What has happened between us, and our families, since he left me has seen to that.

Tara

19

Jason and I were hardly talking when I went into hospital to have my Caesarian on 14 November, seven weeks after he walked out. He had phoned saying he wanted to know how the pregnancy was going, but I found his calls too upsetting and told him I didn't want him to ring.

I had mixed feelings about him being at the birth. When I woke up that morning, though, I was quite frightened about delivering my first child and I wanted him there. I arranged for Kim Dixon to bring him to the hospital.

When he came into my room, we chatted and inevitably the conversation turned to our separation. He said he had been in touch with his lawyer.

'I've got no money,' he said. 'I'm broke.'

I was enraged he could come out with this sort of stuff at a time like this. It was just as well a nurse came in to wheel me to the birthing suite soon afterwards or I'd have blown a fuse.

I left Jason outside the ante-room to the operating theatre and got Mum to hold my hand to try to calm me down.

Yet Jason was the first to hold our small but perfectly formed 3.5-kilogram girl when she came into the world—I was still recovering from the anaesthetic.

When I came to, I went upstairs to the newborn babies' ward. Mum, Kim and Jason were there, but as soon as my eyes fell on my baby daughter it was as if the two of us were the only human beings in existence. I couldn't believe the power of the feelings that swept through me. The nurse handed her to me and it was the most natural thing in the world to have her suckle to me, almost melting back into the body she had come from. The power of nature is an amazing thing. Although I had never been conscious of the maternal instinct, from that moment I knew I would give my life to protect my baby girl. The joy and the love I felt for her was so intense it was numbing.

'She's so beautiful, so beautiful,' was all I could say as she settled off to sleep in my arms.

I could see lots of myself as a baby in her—my eyes, my nose, my chin.

I don't know how long I had been in my new-mother trance before I became aware Jason was there. He said his mother and sister were downstairs and they wanted to come up to see the baby. I told him I'd prefer they didn't right then, I was too tired.

Mum went down to see them but it didn't calm the waters.

The next morning a nurse brought Tara to me early in the morning. She'd slept right through the night without a peep, the nurse said. I snuggled her in next to me, still in awe of the close bond I felt to her.

Jason and I had agreed on Tara as a name, after Tara Fisher, my girlhood friend from the pony club. Initially, we had Ann pencilled in as her middle name—both our mothers' middle names were Ann. Later I realised that would leave her with the initials T.A.B., which could be a bit embarrassing for a child from a racing family, so I put her middle name down as Louise, which was my grandmother's middle name.

Tara Louise was asleep when she was brought in to me that morning. I left her briefly to go to the toilet and when I came back, Jason was in the room with a video camera.

'What are you doing here?' I said.

'The father can come in whenever he likes,' he said.

'I'd prefer if you came during visiting hours please,' I replied.

He stormed off. Two days later, among the cards and letters from well-wishers, was a very business-like envelope. It was from Jason's lawyers. They were demanding Jason's family be allowed access to Tara and foreshadowing Jason's claim for a share of our marital property. I found this very upsetting.

The next day Jason turned up the heat another notch. Splashed on the front page of *The Advocate* newspaper was a photograph of Tara, taken from Jason's video footage.

Under the headline 'Dad's anguish over daughter', the article told how 'proud father Jason King' was unable to sleep because of his concern 'he will not be able to see (Tara) again'. Having consulted lawyers, Jason must have known this was absolute rubbish—there is no way I could have cut off his access to Tara even if I had wanted to.

A second front-page picture showed Jason and his father standing over an empty cot. In the article, Jason said he was upset that Kim had been allowed to see Tara straight after the birth but 'so far none of my family has been welcome'.

Towards the end of the article, Jason said: 'There is no hope for the marriage at all now, I'm not in love with Bev any more. I still love her because you can't spend six-and-a-half years with someone who is the mother of your child and not feel anything, but I'm not in love with her.'

He said the final straw was 'when there was trouble about him attending his father's sixtieth birthday party'.

I'm not sure why he made so much of this. I had been reluctant to go to the party, in August, but Jason and I both went in the end.

I was stunned Jason had brought in the heavy legal armoury so quickly. When it became apparent Jason wasn't coming back, I had asked him if he would agree to let me keep the Magna we had in joint names, now that I no longer had the Celica he had written off. I said I would need a reliable, safe car for transporting our child and he signed the transfer of ownership forms quite willingly. 'No problems,' he said.

Since that first lawyer's letter after Tara was born, there have been nothing but problems. Big ones. After I asked Jason to come only during visiting hours, he didn't return to see Tara and I at the hospital. When I took Tara home the following week, a second lawyer's letter arrived seeking official contact rights as if I'd said he wouldn't be allowed to come and see her at Brigadoon. I'd said no such thing.

So I had to hire a lawyer to make an official reply. We came to an arrangement that Jason could come to Brigadoon three times a week for an hour to see Tara. His parents could visit every fortnight, but after one visit his father stopped coming. Often when Jason came, Tara would be asleep and he would leave well before the hour was up. A couple of times I had to change the visiting day because of nursing appointments, but I always allowed him to come the following day instead. When he came over in the third week of December we had a big row, which set the scene for another round of legal letters over arrangements for Christmas.

Jason asked to have Tara at his parents' house on Christmas Day. I said no—she was only six weeks old and I didn't want her to be separated from me when she was still dependent on breastfeeding. The stand-off had to be settled in court: Jason and his parents were granted two hours with Tara on Christmas Day at our place, but with me not in the room. Later the visiting schedule was changed to Jason seeing Tara every day, alternately one day at our house and the next day at his parents' house.

Initially when Jason and I spoke on the phone or face-to-face we could be open and civil with each other, even though we didn't agree. Whenever something had to be formalised through lawyers' letters, all the goodwill and trust seemed to disappear. I don't know if it is the lawyers' fault or just that people aren't brave enough to say what they really mean when they have to confront you in person, but as soon as our dealings went onto legal letterhead, things became inflamed, the room for compromise shrank and a new frontier of battle opened up.

The stress these legal battles caused me changed my feelings towards Jason—if he could do this to me, then he couldn't have loved me that much. He continued to press for a property settlement, including my one-third share in Brigadoon.

Jason's accident, Tara's birth and the split-up had put the planned move to Victoria on the backburner, but in August 2001, almost a year after Jason walked out, Dad spotted a property that would be perfect for us. It was in Benalla, less than one kilometre from the racecourse, with nice flat, open paddocks and buildings that could be converted to stables. Dad flew over for the auction with a strict bidding limit, but he got it for much less than we thought and the sellers agreed to a long settlement. Still, we would have to sell Brigadoon to pay for it, so it became important to settle Jason's claim.

The custody and property settlement hearing was held in February 2002. When it comes to emotional trauma, I'd take being in an intensive care unit over a Family Court case every time. The law forbids anyone from revealing what is said within the courtroom walls, but I am allowed to say this: after being cross-examined over the most intimate and raw details of my personal life, I felt so humiliated and betrayed I could hardly think straight. I just wanted it to end. I agreed to make a payout to Jason and to foot the bills for Tara to fly back to Tasmania to visit him after we moved to Victoria. I would accept financial responsibility for her until she started kindergarten.

As soon as the settlement was finalised, Mum and I joined Dad at Benalla, although it took another eight months to find a buyer for Brigadoon.

From the first day I passed through the white-painted wagon wheels at the entrance to the driveway of our new home in Benalla, it was as if a sky full of storm clouds had been blown away to clear blue. The fresh start I had dreamed of two years before—when Dad and I walked the home straight at Benalla racecourse the day after Becky's brave Oaks run—had finally arrived.

From our place you can look as far as the eye can see in every direction and not spot another house. The vista of flat, open land is broken only by a few trees and fence lines until you hit the high country mountains. The district is very much thoroughbred territory, boasting some of the State's leading stud farms, such as Vinery and Blue Gum at Euroa, and busy racetracks, including Bendigo and Seymour.

Our closest neighbours are native birds, horses and a few Murray Grey calves Mum bought as pets. For me, growing up in this sort of natural, open setting created a feeling that there were no boundaries in life—it was there for the taking. I want the same environment for Tara, and she shows every sign of loving it as much as I did.

She's a dream child despite being a typically strong-willed Scorpio and from the day she was born, she's been a solid sleeper. She's a happy girl, too, although I wonder how much she has sensed of my emotional unrest during my pregnancy and her infancy. Outwardly it doesn't seem to have affected her, except after some of her trips to stay with Jason. He has had a few girlfriends since we split and they have been very helpful in making arrangements for Tara's needs, likes and dislikes when she visits her father. However, any child would find a regular change in home environment unsettling.

She's tough though, and brave, and I think she will get through whatever life throws at her. When she went to the doctor to have her standard injections at eighteen months, she watched the needle go into her thigh and gave him a big smile when the tip came out. The doctor said he'd never seen that before. 'Lolly,' she said, opening the palm of her hand.

When she falls or bangs into something, she pauses to check the pain level before deciding if it is bad enough to justify crying. One day she was scuttling around the lounge room when she tripped on a cushion and fell onto a window sill, splitting the bridge of her nose. There was blood all over her face instantly, but she waited until the full quota of pain registered until she cried, and then it was only until the worst of it subsided. The next day she pointed to her swollen nose and, as if to apologise for causing a fuss, said, 'Hurt, Mummy'.

Like me as a little girl, she can only look at a television screen for a few minutes before she gets bored. She'd much rather be outside playing with the dogs, splashing around in the paddling pool or clambering up the backyard fence.

She seems to have inherited my handyman streak too, and a willingness to get stuck in around the property. I was nailing some wood together one day when she gathered up a loose nail and poked it into a hole in a piece of timber, then grabbed a hammer and carefully tapped it in. She had obviously picked up the technique from watching me. We've had to get her a little wheelbarrow and a rake for the stables, because when she sees me cleaning out the horse boxes she has to pitch in and help. I let her fill the horses' water buckets until she starts squirting me with the hose.

Of course, when it came to learning to walk I was something of an expert teacher. By the time she was ten months, she could toddle along holding my hand, but she wasn't game to let go. Two weeks before her first birthday I took her down the hallway, gradually easing my hand out of hers until she was walking on her own without realising it. When she'd gone about 5 metres I couldn't contain myself and burst out with a round of applause. Tara looked around and suddenly her face lit up as it hit home she was walking under her own steam. From then on she wanted to walk everywhere on her own—she loved it. She had no idea how lucky she was.

Having Tara was the best thing to ever happen to me. I have good days and bad days with my body and my moods, but when I'm with Tara not an hour goes by when I don't experience the unique joy of motherhood. Looking after her comes so naturally, I just automatically sense her feelings and her needs—it's as if she's part of me. Watching her personality take shape and seeing her learn things for the first time is the most wonderful thing, similar to the buzz of seeing a horse's character develop, but so much more intimate and powerful.

The biggest bonus of not being able to work as hard as I used to is that I haven't missed a minute of Tara growing up; her first steps, her first words, putting her down for a sleep each afternoon, reading my childhood favourites like *Robert the Rose Horse* to her.

I don't think she appreciates yet that I'm different to other mothers. I have to insist she holds my hand all the time whenever we leave the property, because I can't move quickly enough to catch her if she walks out into traffic or wanders close to a steep riverbank. Sometimes we'll be in a park and she'll want to take off, pulling on my arm, saying, 'Run Mummy, run.' I have to say, 'Sorry Tara, Mummy can't run.'

Since she turned two, she has become more aware of her surroundings—the possibility of, say, falling over on gravel or getting lost in a crowd—so she sticks close to me, which makes things a little easier.

She's very intelligent for her age—I suppose every mother thinks that—and as far as I'm concerned she can grow up to be whatever she chooses.

Getting back on the horse

My alarm clock goes off at 5.30 a.m. Time to go to work.

I swing my legs out of bed and shuffle into the bathroom, take a quick shower, comb my hair, brush my teeth and go back to the bedroom to get dressed. I don't have the strength and balance to stand on one leg to pull on a pair of jeans, so I have to put them on sitting down. I wear loose shirts— my weak stomach muscles give me a flabby tummy—and doing up the buttons with my stiff fingers takes about ten times longer than before my fall. I'm better at doing up shoe laces because the finger work required is not as tricky.

I have to go to the toilet as soon as I feel the urge— I can't hold on. This makes me a bit nervous when I go out socially so I'm careful not to drink too much.

Because my body's thermometer is still slow to react to heat or cold, the house is temperature-controlled, but on cold mornings it takes a while to kick in and my legs ache like I have bad arthritis until they get warmed up.

In the pre-dawn dimness, I dodge past sleeping dogs and Tara's toys to the front sliding door, gently pull it shut and walk the 30 metres to the stables. Dad is usually there a couple of minutes ahead of me, and Mum is on standby if Tara wakes up early.

My legs feel terribly stiff, as if they are weighed down with bags of lead. The right is worse than the left because my right ankle and knee hardly flex. Even when I consciously try to lift and stretch them into a full stride, it's like gravity won't let the leg leave the ground and my foot flops forward just a few inches.

I used to hate the feeling of ungainliness when I walked— a woman in a shop once asked me if I had a wooden leg. Now I've been moving like this for so long that I've got used to it; for me, hobbling is 'normal'. I'm not as self-conscious as I used to be about people staring either, but I wish they would ask me what is wrong rather than act as if I'm a staggering drunk or mentally deranged.

In the early days after I got off crutches, I would study the way people walked and try to work out how to get my stride looking more natural. It took a few months to work out that I was only concentrating on my legs, stabbing them forward like stilts, whereas uninjured people used their hips to roll their strides along.

I worked on the hip movement and it improved my style, but when I overdid it and swung too much, or tried to step too quickly, I would trip over my own feet. The fingers of my right hand still don't open out fully, so when I fall my knuckles and elbows take the impact. I've got my fall rate down a long way from the early days, but every now and then I'll clip my feet on an uneven surface and go down— my knuckles are semi-permanently skinned and my forearms are a mottled dark-brown from the continual bruising.

I don't have full sensation in my limbs, so if I cut my arms or legs I usually see the blood before I feel any pain.

Although my walking is pretty slow and awkward, I have built up my leg muscle stamina and can walk as far as I need to, but never as quickly as I want. On a scale where five is normal, my leg strength is four. I won't lead racehorses around any more because I can't keep up with them, and a decent nudge from a fully grown thoroughbred would sit me on my backside.

My upper body is pretty strong now—I can lift a 30-kilo bag of feed off the ground, although not above my head; my triceps still aren't what they used to be. I will probably end up in a wheelchair again in the long run, because my weakened muscles will deteriorate a lot faster than they would from the normal ageing process.

When I get to the stables, I take the muck out of the boxes and level the sawdust, fill the horses' water tins and mix up their feed. I am naturally right-handed, but I have to use my left for tasks that require a degree of flexibility, such as scooping up handfuls of grain and oats and stirring them together.

When we've done the equine housekeeping, Dad loads the horses doing trackwork that morning onto the float and drives them up to the Benalla racetrack. It's your classic country track, like something you'd see in a colonial era painting, especially when the full morning light hits the gum trees that ring the course.

I drive ahead of Dad and catch up with the gossip from the other half-a-dozen trainers who use the track. Only a couple have reasonable-sized teams—most are just training one or two horses as a hobby—so there is none of the sniping and one-upmanship you can get at bigger tracks where the competition is cut-throat. If your track rider doesn't turn up you can always find someone to help out, or if you're having a problem with a horse that one of the other trainers has a solution for, they'll always volunteer it.

I lay out my little first aid kit—skin creams, anti-bacteria sprays, bandages and hoof ointment—as Dad unloads the three or four horses that need a gallop. Being so hands-on with them, I know all their personalities inside out. I must sound like a fussing mother as I tell Duke, the last survivor of the Brigadoon Boy family, to stop swishing his tail, and then growl at him for biting at my fingers as I slip his bridle on.

Duke is a great grandson of Teragarm, the beautiful black mare who got us off to a flying start in racing more than 25 years ago. We bred Duke from a daughter of Sweet Martia, the half-sister to Brigadoon Boy who gave me windburn when I first started trackriding at Old Beach as a schoolgirl.

Through the generations, however, the Brigadoon Boy bloodline has been watered down. When I swing a saddle onto Duke he arches his back like a child who doesn't want to wear the jumper his mother has just picked out for him. Duke's half-brother was a real handful who put on a rodeo show every time he went to the track, winning his first start but then becoming unmanageable. This little fellow is the opposite—lazy and slow.

Once I've got him saddled, I leg the track rider up and send him off to do a warm-up lap on the dirt track inside the course proper. I walk over to the neat, red-brick grandstand and lean on the rail opposite the winning post to watch Duke head out onto the grass track for his gallop. His rider urges him along but the little bloke is not interested. A slap over the shoulder with the whip as he enters the straight gets his attention, but not for long. He lolls his head off to one side as if to say, 'Did you see that, I'm going to report this', quickening up just enough to avoid another whack from the rider.

I head back to the stalls, ready to unsaddle the lazy bugger and hose him down. 'What are we going to do with you 'Dukey'?' I say, but I get the feeling he's not listening.

I notice he's got a little nick on a back leg, so once he's tethered in his stall I apply some anti-bacterial spray.

As I head off back to the rails to see our next runner gallop, Duke stamps his feet—he wants some more mothering. He needs to be less of a sook if he's going to make a racehorse, so I give him a flick under the belly with a towel and growl, 'Stop it! You know better than that.' He obeys, but drops his head in a sulk.

What are we going to do with you, Dukey?

I haven't given up on the dream of winning a Melbourne Cup; I'll never do it as a jockey, but I might as a trainer.

Since my days as an apprentice, before I knew whether I would have a successful riding career or not, the one certain thing in my future was that I would take over the training reins from Dad. In 1998 I had it all mapped out; two or three more seasons in the saddle, then trade in the riding boots for baby booties, and when the demands of motherhood started to ease, Dad could retire and help me start the next phase of my racing career.

Unitl this year, I had been too consumed with my rehabilitation, losing Jason, having Tara, and the hassles over her custody to think about the future. Now that five-year fog of living in crisis mode has lifted.

In May I took Tara over to Tasmania for one of her three-day visits and I rang Jason to see if we could sort out our differences. He invited me over to dinner. By the end of the night, he was promising to move to Victoria to see more of Tara and lift the burden off me in paying for her flights to Tasmania. He wanted us to get back together, he said. I told him I'd be happy for him to move close enough to be able to see Tara whenever he liked—she loves him dearly. But I am not going to forget how devastating it was when he left me. I said we couldn't be a couple again.

He came over in June to look around for a job and somewhere to live. He booked into a backpacker hostel in Benalla, and I picked him up in the mornings and brought him to our place to see Tara. We all got on so well it was almost like the good old days. After a week Jason went back to Tassie to tidy up his affairs. He sold his house and returned to Victoria in August, to look for somewhere to live not too far from Benalla. I admire him for having the courage to do the right thing by Tara.

Still, I've lost a bit of faith in men, as life partners anyway. I don't know if I could trust one with all my heart again. It took me two years after Jason left to go out dating again. I met a man in Benalla, a former apprentice jockey, who is kind, open and honest, but for my sake, and Tara's, I didn't want it to get too serious. It was great for my self-esteem to know that despite everything I could still be attractive to the opposite sex.

With Jason's move promising to solve the problem of Tara's access visits, I started thinking seriously about taking out my trainer's licence. I know all the negatives the demanding hours and the financial instability—but there are valuable lifestyle benefits that make up for that. I love horses so much that working with them is a pleasure not a chore. And how many other jobs allow you to do half your day's work and still be home in time to have breakfast with your kids?

In July I applied to the Victorian stewards for my trainer's licence and if all goes well I will start training our team in the 2003–04 season. The prospects for lady trainers are a lot better than for female jockeys. The thing owners and trainers can never get past is their obsession with physical strength. With training, the results speak for themselves, so it doesn't matter that Gai Waterhouse or Sheila Laxon can't bench-press as much as Lee Freedman or John Hawkes.

Since I stopped riding, there has been a succession of dedicated, beautifully balanced, tactically astute girls come through and match the best of the young male riders, but they never get the opportunities at the highest level here, as they do in New Zealand. It still makes me furious when I go to the races and hear the snide remarks when a horse ridden by a lady doesn't do as well as an owner thinks it should have. 'The bloody sheila' is always easier to blame than a horse that doesn't put in or a trainer who doesn't take the time to work out how to get the best out of a horse.

Things haven't become any easier for small country trainers in Victoria since we pulled up stumps from Ballarat twelve years ago. Dad started at Benalla with only half-a-dozen clients, some of whom had brought their horses to us after they failed to show ability with other trainers. It takes time to get horses used to our way of doing things and to undo any bad habits they have picked up.

We have a few horses of our own in Benalla, including Naami, a well-bred filly we named in honour of my brilliant physiotherapist and friend from Tassie. Unfortunately Naami the horse has had her own injury problems—ones that only Mother Nature and rest will heal. We've sent some of our retired mares to be mated to stallions in the area to build up the stable, but the babies will also take time to come through. Dad bought a full brother to Becky at the 2003 Melbourne yearling sales for $35 000, money he didn't really have, but after his success with Becky, we'll have no trouble finding owners to take shares in him. Although I'll be starting from humble beginnings, my old ambitiousness has returned, and I want to have as much success as a trainer as I did in the saddle—so watch out, Gai.

In the meantime it's lean pickings. In his first year back in Victoria, Dad had only two winners. He couldn't afford to pay me and I wasn't able to do all the tasks you'd expect of a hired stable-hand—I just helped out where I could.

Between renovating Brigadoon for my rehabilitation, paying Naami and other specialists, and two years' of lawyers' bills dealing with Jason, I've used up all my money, including that from the fundraising appeal. I live on a disability pension of $217 a week and I get a child allowance of about $100 for Tara.

When I was riding I made good money—$40 000 to $50 000 in Tasmania bought a very comfortable lifestyle in the late 1980s and early 1990s. I could buy myself nice clothes, I had my flash black Celica and I could go out wherever, and whenever, I wanted.

If you go through my log book of rides, though, you'll see I wasn't really in it for the money. Apart from the summer carnival, I was often riding in races with total prizemoney of $4000 or $6000. My winning percentage would be $120 or $180, not much for an 80-hour week on a starvation diet, let alone literally risking your neck every day.

Still, when I really think about it, I realise I'm one of the lucky ones. I only have to pick up the paper and read about another jockey being killed or brain damaged in a fall to count my blessings. And then there are all the other 'paras' and 'quads' who haven't been fortunate enough to have the recovery I did.

And I'm in better shape than I might look. I was invited to be guest speaker at the local Thoroughbred Breeders' Association dinner early this year. About 40 people turned up at a function centre in Euroa and the master of ceremonies duly introduced me and asked me to take a seat at the microphone. I enjoy getting out and speaking to racing people, but I am nervous about presenting myself as a public speaker—I prefer to just take questions from the audience.

I didn't get a chance to get nervous this night. When I sat down, the chair collapsed under me and I fell straight to the floor, bum first. The guests sucked in their breath in stunned silence. What if I'd done my neck in again? Even when I started giggling they didn't make a sound. I told the crowd I didn't realise I'd been invited to do a comedy routine.

It took four years from the fall for the urge to ride to take hold of me again.

After three or four months at Benalla, my self-confidence was returning and I hinted to Mum and Dad that if they were to find me a safe old plodder to play around on I wouldn't send it back. Word spread quickly among the horse owners around town, and it didn't take long before we found a woman with a half-Clydesdale mare that was only getting exercise from chewing its food.

We drove around to see the mare and I introduced myself to Dolly, a placid, fat 15-year-old with a white blaze on her nose and white socks. I had to stand on a bucket to get onto her broad back, but once I tucked my feet into the stirrups I felt right at home, as if I hadn't missed a day in the saddle. I tested her out, trotting, cantering and turning her around her yard. She was easy to handle, even when she tried to duck out the gate—I gave her a good dig in the ribs and she didn't try that again.

I was thrilled to find that riding was easier on my legs than walking; because there is hardly any movement required, the stronger muscles can carry the load on their own, so once I'm aboard I've got all the power I need.

I'm confident enough now to take Dolly out along the trails in the bush around our place on my own. I have even put a big, padded stock saddle on a couple of the quieter thoroughbreds and trotted them around the roads. It would be tempting to jump on one at the track and have a flat-out gallop up the straight for old time's sake, but what's the point?—I'll never be able to ride in a race again and all I would be doing is risking another injury.

Dolly was the first horse Tara rode. When I nestled her into my lap and clicked the old mare into stride my daughter's eyes bulged with excitement and wonder, just as mine had when Dad picked me up from school on Dream Valley.

Last Christmas I bought Tara a miniature horse, Robbie, who doubles as a lawnmower for our front yard. I keep a hand on Tara as Robbie quietly walks her around in a circle, but Tara shows no fear. She loves riding. I've noticed the carpark at the local pony club is full of floats whenever it holds its gatherings next to the racecourse, and I can't wait to enrol Tara there.

When the races are on TV, Tara hops on her rocking horse and mimics the riders flailing their whips down the straight. Would I let her become a jockey, knowing what I know now?

Of course. To be a race rider you have to be fearless—you know terrible accidents can happen, but dwelling on that, second-guessing your instincts, only makes a disaster more likely. It's the same in life. If you let fear get the better of you, you have no life. That's what I'm trying to teach Tara. I'm going to make sure, as I reshape my own future, she learns it from what I practise, not just what I preach.

Index

The initials BB stand for Beverley Buckingham; JK stands for Jason King.

34967767R00176

Printed in Great Britain
by Amazon